The Small Book

How I Beat Alcoholism And Why
Alcoholics Anonymous Doesn't Work

By

Charles Hurst

ISBN: 9798597130460 (paperback)

*To Bill and Bob. It was a good idea that should have evolved.
It's now time that it did.*

TABLE OF CONTENTS

CHAPTER 1

THE DUTCH UNCLE

June 1986

The air was warm the night of graduation. Norfolk Catholic High would soon be my teenage alma mater, where I had resided the last year and a half.

Norfolk had been my transplanted home for fifteen months. I use the word "home" lightly. Like many firstborn of dysfunctional families, I had paid the price, a sacrificial lamb, whose blood alleviated the burden of their failed responsibilities as parents. And they had pulled me from a boiling pot only to toss me into a blazing fire. I was placed with a horrid grandmother who took a personal interest in the reiteration, during my time there, that the exploded nuclear familial factory in Cincinnati was my doing alone. Miserable doesn't even begin to describe my time in Norfolk.

Society was different in 1986. This was especially true in the arena of the under-aged and their ability to obtain alcohol illegally. In those days, there weren't special seals on the drivers' licenses that a bright light could easily verify. Nightclubs didn't have a book of what every state license looked like either. These were the days when the doorman only gave a cursory glance at the age and identification on a card that may have been ordered from a rock music magazine. The era when the judge's gavel may slap a few hundred dollars for a first offense D.U.I. People had a bit more sense back then. Sure, youth periodically drank when they could render a quick date with Jack London's friend, John Barleycorn, on a Saturday night while the parents were out. But it wasn't thoroughly abused. And as long as kids weren't placing their dads' cars into the Chesapeake Bay, a *see no evil* philosophy was applied.

The high school students, waiting for the gates of adulthood to open, didn't overexploit their late-night companion, and generally sent him back home at the proper hour. As they probably did in earlier times as well. But they still had to finagle a way to call their cohort out. At seventeen, I had acquired a "fake I.D." from an old, black man who ran a photo shop downtown. I was directed to his small building by word of mouth from a peer of mine. The I.D. was ridiculous. It read *Personal Identification* and gave no specific state of origin. It was about as fake and illegitimate as it could be for the fifteen dollars I paid for the laminated plastic. Before the old-timer had given it to me, he altered the information card I had scribbled for him prior to the snapshot.

"Had to change your zip code, son," he said. I looked at him perplexed, both of us pretending that we had no clue why I was sitting in his studio. "Your zip says you're from Minnesota."

"Oh," I stammered. Being a white boy, my flush was apparent. I was going to have to buy a better poker face if I was going to play this game in the liquor stores. The legal grandfathered drinking age at the time was nineteen. He chuckled and handed the validation that stated I was two years older than my seventeen spins that were displayed on my real license. Apparently, I wasn't the first kid who thought he was streetwise, sitting in front of the adult, who actually was, in this establishment.

I walked out, flush dissipating from my cheeks, replaced by a new swagger as I strolled downtown back to my pickup truck. I was completely illegitimately legit. And the I.D. worked everywhere I went. Today, it wouldn't have—not even for a second. But back then it sure did. I'm sure nobody believed the I.D. was real. They just didn't care. I was only questioned one time when I resupplied the beer for a party after the end of the school year. I had self-isolated myself the entire time there, so parties were a rarity for me. Suddenly, the I.D. guy was immensely popular among his classmates for the very short time I stayed. I was in the grocery store with Cecil, who was six foot and well over two hundred and fifty pounds, on his way to college ball. The clerk scanned both of us with our cases of beer in front of him. It wasn't Cecil he questioned.

"Where's your driver's license?" he demanded. He motioned for the store manager. This time the flush wasn't there as I was a seasoned criminal. I had kept a bottle of vodka, which I rarely touched, in my school locker. It seemed to add to my perceived aura of outlawishness, which registered with no one except myself. I looked at both of them when the manager came over.

"They took it—my regular license. I got a few D.U.I.s," I said. That was spur of the moment brilliant, I thought, keeping my eyes level. I could be pretty sharp when I wanted.

"You in the service?"

"Marines." I gave my best thousand-yard stare at seventeen. This bald-faced lie was slightly plausible as I was built like a Marine and there was a Marine detachment stationed at the naval base in Norfolk. Sometimes I was a clever kid. Of course, if they had looked up and asked me why my address on the I.D. didn't match the barracks address on the base or why my hair was a little long for the service, I would have been out of bright ideas of explanation. They didn't. Cecil and I carried out the cases of beer. I was popular for about a minute with my peers when we returned. I didn't stay too long or overindulge that night.

But I had determined the night of graduation, I was going to get smashed. I hadn't wanted to even go to graduation. I didn't have any friends as I was a misfit who had been tossed out of his home. I just wanted to leave the whole city without notice. But my grandmother would have none of it. We must give the illusion everything is peachy, even if you're biting into a lemon. And my parents had come down and brought a childhood friend from Indiana. There was another party after the mundane ceremony. It was either that or hang out with my dysfunctional family.

Leah was throwing the bash at her parents' house. As I said, things were simpler back then. We were to deposit our car keys in a jar until the following morning. Her neighbors would recognize one unruly, loud night, where teenagers were drinking illegally, and it would pass without calling in the authorities.

The problem with the first major drunk is it never goes well for the participant. I had only taken nips here and there up until then. The most I had consumed was three beers to diffuse the social phobia I had developed during high school. This illegal act occurred during a rare outing with a few members of my football team, which had led to a buzz that lasted for over an hour afterward.

I was quite terrified of groups, even if I had been invited nicely to mix in with them. But I had managed to complete my secondary education. Something I wasn't sure I would finish a few months prior. So I was going to drink hard that night. I would tragically celebrate the end of the miserable experience I had endured over the last four years. I don't think I wanted to get drunk as much as I just wanted to get numb.

I prepped the party by sitting in my rusty Toyota truck, a block away, and put down three bottles of beer. It was malt liquor beer which was the "in" thing to drink for underage, wannabee adults in 1986. The first liquid Yuletides began to flow as I stepped into the celebration. There were kegs already open. Leah took my keys, and I was on my way. The former students were passing around a bottle of vodka as well. Why not, I had that criminal career of the rarely touched bottle in my locker, after all. And I was feeling pretty fine now. Suddenly, I couldn't imagine why I had avoided such get-together events before.

But the answer was simple. The reason that I had intermingled with my classmates only a few times up to graduation. Before entering Norfolk Catholic, I had been a member of the illustrious and prestigious all-boys' school of Saint Xavier in Cincinnati, Ohio. When I started my freshman year, I weighed about a hundred pounds, my frame topped with nerdy, wire-rim glasses. Add that to my eccentric personality, and I was instantly a designated target.

To say I was picked on would be an understatement. I was terrorized by several packs of boys during those years. Added to the fear of living at home, the situation had become intense enough that I was taken to the doctor several times for non-specified stomach pain. Imagine being a fourteen-year-old, slinking from classroom to classroom in a constant state of fright. And then going home and hiding in your room. The years fourteen to sixteen were a time of living in perpetual fear. That period would set a precedent to an adulthood which would attempt rectification by throwing the victim into a river of barley.

At fourteen, I had discovered bodybuilding with weights. And it became an obsession. By sixteen, abuse at school only came in packs now. Individually, they weren't so sure as I had gotten a lot bigger over the last two years. But the damage had been done. If only I had started my freshman year with the ability to bench press two hundred pounds, as I could at sixteen, things may have been different. But I didn't start that way. My peers remembered the first impression of me, which was ingrained the entire time I was at Saint Xavier.

When I transferred to Norfolk Catholic, I left under violent circumstances. The first bully I stood up to was my father. Suddenly, he wasn't terrifying anymore. He was smaller than me by my junior year. And I was filled with an almost murderous rage. The problems with my abusive father had only escalated during the almost three years at my first high school.

My grade point average at Saint Xavier had plummeted from a half point shy of First Honors, my first semester, to a sixty-eight percent my last graded period at the school during my junior year. And I had a growing list of demerits that would soon lead to expulsion if I stayed. If I had had a decent father, he would have seen what was happening. After all, it happened to him as well when he was in school. The only thing my father cared about was grades, not because he was concerned for my future but because it reflected on him in his mind. We were a well to do family where superficial coatings were of far greater value than the rusted metal underneath. During a final argument, I threatened to put him through a wall. And for the first time, I comprehended what a bully understood.

Fear.

When I entered Norfolk Catholic toward the tail end of my junior year, I was well received. I looked like an athlete now, wiry glasses replaced by contacts. I was even on the football team. It was third-string only at the small, single A division, but I was accepted as part of it. And I was invited to all of the after-game parties. But I went to the movie cinema instead on the weekends. Alone, petrified to interact with my peers, even though they were friendly to me. This phobia was aftereffect anxiety at work.

I cannot say I was picked on at Norfolk Catholic, although within a few months, it was evident to the other students that something was wrong with me. One tried to start a rendition of Saint Xavier. I let it go for a day. Then I challenged him to a fight after school, even though I probably would have lost the altercation. Because I had learned it was better to fight and lose than run away. He never showed, and it never happened again.

I didn't spend the last year of high school in fear. It passed only in isolation. And this time the prison was self-induced. It wasn't the other boys' fault this round. Teenagers aren't adults. They aren't mature enough to understand post-trauma. And I wasn't old enough to get over it yet. A lot of them didn't even know that I had left home and that I was actually from Cincinnati my last stop. They only understood that one of their peers had snubbed them. So they returned the favor indifferently. That's what kids do. I stayed clear of the Homecoming Dance and all the post-game parties. By the time senior prom came, no one even questioned whether I would be going. I was a complete outcast from the rest of the class. I ate lunches alone and counted the days for high school to end.

But the night of Leah's party, I wasn't isolated. I felt grand as the spirit and barley took hold. *So this was what it was like to be social. This wasn't so bad,* I thought. As a matter of fact, I felt so terrific, I thought I should pour even more down my gullet. I was mixing the vodka and beer—the telltale sign of a true novice. And we all know the outcome of a neophyte when he collides roughly with man's second oldest vice.

To declare I was sick a few hours later would be stating the matter lightly. I'm certain Death was notified of a potential client and was walking down the sidewalk toward me. I spent most of the night being lectured about marrying Mother Russia with Dutch Uncle Bud through a series of violent retching while I lay immobilized on the back lawn outside. My only consolation was I could hear Big Mike, from our football team, in the same classroom about thirty feet away. If only youth could read the CliffsNotes on the valuable lessons of life instead of having to suffer through the entire book. But youth is youth. I would lie on the lawn in a semi-delirium until around 7 a.m. the next morning, finally being able to stand on unsteady legs as my childhood pal, who came to the party with me, drove us back home.

I felt like Dante had taken a personal interest and sent me to the second or third level that morning. No one forgets the first hangover. I am astounded that the indulgence that causes it has stayed in existence due to the effect. It looked a lot more fun on *Animal House*. Breakfast was out of the question. If I had anything left in my stomach, it would have come up immediately as severe nausea persisted while the smell of bacon in my grandmother's kitchen only amplified the symptoms. My family asked how much I drank the night before. I told the expected lie, that no one believed, uttered from a pale countenance, which feebly verbalized that I "had a few." On top of which, I got to engage in my final chore for my grandmother of cleaning the roof gutters. The damp, rotting leaves I attempted to bend over and remove made my head swirl even further as I began to fear I would pass out and topple off. Jerry did most of the work while I lay on the top of the house, counting the agonizing minutes to the day's end. Surely, this had to pass? I swore to my neglected Shepherd and most of my deceased ancestors that I would never touch alcohol again.

The next morning, our two-car caravan was en route back to Cincinnati. My father was much friendlier to me now. Of course, I was even bigger than when

I left. And I had completed high school, which a year ago wasn't guaranteed. I still felt ill and finally took a few bites of food during the stops. Even forty-eight hours later, I was aware of a mild queasiness that came on with the thought of the graduation bottle. Only on the third day after my misadventure, back in Cincinnati, would I claim normality once again. I praised the angels above that I had survived the encounter.

When I returned to Cincinnati, I got a job at a restaurant and immediately made friends for the first time in four years. One of them was Jim, a quirky, short guy who became a comrade until his death from cancer at forty-nine years old. He worked the salad bar, and I was in the drive thru as well as a dishwasher. And he introduced me to his pack. Suddenly, I had gone from a high school recluse to a normal, interacting, late-year teenager about to cross the current to the rougher waters of adulthood. I had an incredibly fun summer and was a year away from being a competitive bodybuilder.

My oath lasted only a few weeks. We drank that summer. Beer mainly as I had already been well-schooled in the hardened, white liquid phantoms, which I was now okay with leaving in the haunted attics. I approached the first night out with Jim and his pals with trepidation, starting with only sips of my former poison. I found that with leisure stride, I could gain the same anesthetic effect without the violent aftermath. Sure, we had hangovers but nothing like on the lawn of Leah's house during the early morning following graduation. Four cups of coffee after two hours of sleep could get us through the shift at the restaurant the next day. And once I figured out how to manage the hangover, it became a regular part of my life. Sometimes one morning was more severe in symptoms, depending upon our intensity the night before, but never like my first failed experiment. I had already stepped through the rite of passage.

And I had unlocked the door to addiction. The demon had waited patiently for the key to turn. And when the beast stepped through it was in no hurry. It could take the terrain slowly. There was a difference between myself and Jim and his friends. They were drinking because they were typical and reckless young adults. I was using it to numb pain. I was still short but very powerfully built now. And I had ventured in the beginnings of what would be a long martial arts career. No one would have guessed this was the same body that fled from classroom to classroom at Saint Xavier only a few years before. I had become obsessed with physical toughness and bodybuilding. But emotionally, I was still fourteen, whose soul remained frozen from the past trauma.

I had no social skills, which translates to no dating skills. I had the largest arms of anyone in my peer group but never went out with the opposite sex, exhibiting an awkwardness which drove the female in the opposite direction. I had managed about three dates from eighteen to twenty-one. None of them had gone past the first encounter. I carried an aura of tenseness matched with severe lack of inner confidence—a combination not endearing at all to women. I repelled them and didn't know why—after all, I was the athlete of the group.

The trauma from childhood had silently carried over into adulthood—stowed away while the ship crossed the river and then quietly strolled off the plank to the shoreline with me. It looked at the new land and decided to conquer it. And it offered the numbing agent while it hammered the stakes in over the years, convincing me the fortress being built was for protection and not the prison it resembled. It proposed the friendship that lacked in high school and the companionship that was absent now. It held out the bottle, brothers in arms in an unfair world where all wrongs were rectified. The demon walked through the door, stretched its legs and set its stride toward my new countryside.

CHAPTER 2

THE ABYSS

August 2008

It was a Monday night. The time was approximately 9:00 p.m. Severe agitation quaked through every fiber of my being as I tried to sleep. Pins and needles stabbed at my right side and back. Notices from the liver and kidneys, pinpricking and alerting of the daily detox, which was beginning as I prepared to return to work the next day. When I stood, the room spun with vertigo as my temples pounded. I would have to put two or three down to re-stabilize before I called the end of the long weekend binge.

I had just come off four days of continuous drinking and had finished almost three cases of beer during the past ninety-six hours. I was on a contract as a physical therapist at a hospital in Redding, California. I worked four, ten-hour days a week, which meant that many times, I had three or four days off in a row. This weekend was one of them. It was a mini-vacation from Thursday night until Tuesday morning. I had left work at 6:00 p.m. on Thursday. I was into my first can of the hops fifteen minutes later. For the next few nights, the only time I left the apartment was to resupply the intoxicant.

I drank every night now. Heavily. It hadn't started that way many years before. It never does with alcoholic addiction. After my initial high school encounter, I had kept the consumption with only my friends in Cincinnati a few days a week. But even then it was never in moderate amounts. Getting smashed in those days was accomplished with seven or eight dead soldiers on the barley field. I was in the nymph stages back then.

The first major protracted binge that I indulged in was during my first year in the active military. I was twenty-two years old. I had initially gone to the Defense Language Institute for the U.S. Army. Prior to those years, before full enlistment, my parents had gotten divorced. My mother had attempted suicide shortly after and ended up in a mental institution for a brief stay while her new boyfriend sat at home unemployed. A sense of entitlement was beginning to come from all of them as I was the only one who held a job in the cramped apartment. Even if my occupation was just as an unskilled laborer with a moving company. I was already in the Army Reserve. This chaos that surrounded me would eventually lead me to the recruiter's office once again.

I had transitioned to a broken down efficiency on my own, funded by the upward mobility of achieving a position as a correctional officer for the Hamilton County Sheriff's Department for 8.64 an hour. A job which gave me a dollar and fourteen cents an hour more than what I was earning lifting furniture out of peoples' houses every day. I had this notion of trying to finish college, having no idea what degree would get me out of the wretched domain on Harrison Ave.

And I just wanted to leave them all behind. It was obvious my mother wasn't going to be able to handle life well on her own, and I didn't want to be near what would be continuous chaos in a town that held nothing but horrible memories. The army had provided the final escape route from Cincinnati. I never lived there again once I got on the plane for California with my duffel bags, already packed with camouflage from the reserves. I had taken the oath of the patriotic and desperate for active duty.

The problem with trying to run away is the person running is usually the common denominator from the origin of the problem, even if now located across the country. I've seen this many times in the military—catastrophic childhoods fled from, only to realize the iron strings to the crisis are still firmly attached, the hooks buried deep into the flesh. This holds true, even if you are transplanted to sunny Monterey. I was twenty-two but still had the mentality of a fifteen-year-old. There remained the traumatized child, frozen in time. And children tend to throw tantrums.

I picked petty fights with the higher-ups continuously. Firefights over polishing boots and pressing uniforms. Or the inconvenience of shining brass, which takes about ten minutes. I excelled at bringing firepower to wars that had never been declared. I had signed on to Military Intelligence, which sent me to my first station at the Defense Language School. I managed to get thrown out of the first Polish class, get recycled to the next one and was verging on getting tossed from the downsizing army altogether. The unhappy life I thought I had left behind stayed with me. And my self-induced habit of anesthesia was at the liquor section from the PX up the hill, which I visited every day after class to numb my ills away.

I did manage to graduate from the language school in June of 1992. My next course to become fully qualified as a member of Intelligence, which I was finding more oxymoronic the longer my enlistment progressed, was located at Goodfellow Air Force base. During the summer there, the drinking tapered back to recreational use. I gazed at my time in Monterey only as a prolonged hiccup in sobriety that had fully resolved now. There was only periodic use of the barely at Fort Devens, Massachusetts as well, during the last course of my training. But whenever I touched it, I drank large quantities. I was setting the foundation where the immense amounts would one day be a nightly habit.

From the Fort Devens training course, I managed to slip across the base and volunteer for a SOT-A team. This was a significant move as it wasn't regular MI but an illustrious group of Intelligence soldiers that fell out of planes, carried a hundred pounds on their backs, and set up radio reconnaissance sites in remote operational areas. A team like this was exactly what I was hoping for in the military. Unconventional, which was a good thing as I don't think I would have lasted in the regular army MI. My recollection of the SOT-A's was that we did indeed all drink hard but trained hard as well. Most of my time was spent in rigorous physical fitness activity to stay on the team. But there was now steady drinking as well while the two years at Fort Devens passed.

When I left the military at twenty-six, the alcohol intake seemed to decrease once again. I rode out of Fort Devens on my Harley with a notion of gaining access into physical therapy school—a profession which would finally break me out of the underclass I had lived in for years. I continued weight lifting and martial arts and only drank heavily about twice a week—usually stemming from a violent town nightclub I worked at as a bouncer and bartender in Bloomington, Indiana. The intake, however, seemed to be in a state of maintained control. The addiction will do that—lull one into a comfortable stride as it leads the victim right to the ambush further down the trail.

In the spring of 1996, it happened. I was twenty-seven and doing very well in my second semester of college. It appeared as if I *would* be competitive for applying to the physical therapy program in Indianapolis. I never really comprehended that I would have medical initials next to my name in a much more civilized venue. During our semester spring break, I decided to celebrate my future aspirations with a visit to my army ex-team member, Joel, who was at a language course in Washington D.C. Mainly, I wanted to get the hell away from college students for a week as I was as comfortable with them as a wet sock in the winter.

The demon, who had been walking with me at a leisure pace, suddenly yanked me into the dark caverns. For a week straight, I drank every night and most of the days. I figured I would go back to controlled intake once back in school. I didn't—not this time. Alcohol had been dickering with me back and forth for years now. And it finally led me to hostile terrain, well past enemy lines. By the time I realized I didn't recognize the landscape, I was already captured.

My second year of college consisted of a light course load as my service in the military nullified many required elective credits. So I had time to make the grades in the few courses I had and still drink heavily at night. When I got my letter of acceptance for the entrance into the physical therapy program in Indianapolis, they were most likely unaware they had just accepted a moderate stage alcoholic into their school.

The progression of addiction continued to work in stages. And I had just advanced myself to the pros. There was no more semi-maintained, periodic, binge drinking. I drank almost every night now. Many nights it was just a six-pack. Sometimes it was eight beers. Weekends always consisted of much more. The experts would call me a functioning alcoholic, I imagine. I still studied a lot in physical therapy school. And I was physically very active. I had switched from traditional martial arts to full contact Thai boxing. I had my first of many school-sponsored fights while in PT school. But I was drinking almost every night. Every morning was a hangover. I am astounded to this day that I was even able to study and graduate from the physical therapy program at all. By my senior year, I knew I had a serious problem with alcohol.

At thirty-one, I graduated from the program. Then the field managed to collapse due to budget cuts in Medicare. On top of that, I failed the boards—twice. This catastrophe resulted in the delay of my practice for two years. However, I did manage to finally get my license once I got my mental priorities in order and ceased Thai boxing for six months while I studied for the boards. I was now drinking two cases of beer a week. At thirty-one, I had suspected that I was an alcoholic as I picked up my degree in the mail. By thirty-three, now a licensed practitioner, I knew it for sure. And I didn't care.

The two years between graduating the program and getting licensed was when the alcoholism made its progression once again to a new plateau. I had fallen into a suicidal, black depression. I spent those two years helping to run the Thai boxing gym as an assistant instructor, fighting in the school bouts every two or three months and fueling my endeavors through addiction every single night. I lived in the ghetto, a tiny, one-room studio. When the lights were flipped on at night, the roaches would scurry back underneath the counter.

If the constant intake and withdrawal hadn't clouded my vision, I would have had the boards wrapped up in a few months. It wasn't that difficult—in the end, all I had to do was take a course in Chicago over one weekend that instructed how to pass the test. That's what I did when I finally put the Thai boxing on hold and, lo and behold, was holding my license in my hand shortly afterward. But my life was chaos until I did, those few years post-graduation. Intermittent women drifted in and out of my efficiency—the type of female that follows fighters. It isn't a good species. But I had status in the Thai boxing school with that blur of pretty women. I didn't want to leave it. My judgment was impaired. I can only describe those two years as a haze that cleared only slightly when I got my license. When I finally did, I left Indianapolis a month later for good.

My first physical therapist job was in Sellersburg, Indiana, a hundred miles away from Indianapolis. At this time, I should have quit the barley and reconstructed my life. Overnight, I had escaped poverty forever. I was now in the medical field as a provider. But the demon had already driven in its stakes, and the ground had hardened like cement around them.

The problem with professionals in the medical field is most of them inwardly deem themselves better than the rest of society. This attitude, I imagine, is because of niceties collected and initials next to their names on their silly clipped tags at the hospitals and clinics. But the white-collar has the stains of addiction as well. Doctors sometimes become addicted to drugs. I once knew a nurse who lost her license for burglary—the origin of the offense was to supply her heroin habit. Here is the uncomfortable fact they would rather I not state out loud. *We aren't any different than anyone else.* We just took a few science courses. I had my initials as well—P.T. Everyone regarded me as a good therapist. But I was a raging alcoholic the hours I wasn't one.

I continued to Thai box from Indiana to California. A crushed cervical nerve injury ended my thoughts of going pro when I was almost thirty-five. It took nine months to recover the full tricep strength in my right arm. I still practiced the art but not nearly with the volume required to compete. Suddenly, I had more time to relieve the cans and bottles of their contents. I stayed at about two cases a week. Every once in a while, I would drink just two or four a night to prove that I had everything under control. I continued to convince myself that I could always go back to being a moderate drinker. And I would be for a few days to a week. And then it was back to normal, which for the alcoholic is everything but normality.

The only saving grace I had was I never drank at work. And I rarely touched the hard stuff. I didn't need to with the amount of beer I was putting away at a hundred and fifty-pound body weight. The hangovers seemed less intense as I was well used to them. It wasn't 1986 graduation night anymore. Two cups of coffee, a bottle of Gatorade, half a lunch a few hours later, and I was ready to roll through until my next stop at the liquor store on the way home.

I don't believe in denial. This proclamation would be my first contention with the AA philosophy that continuously and condescendingly rants about that river in Egypt. An alcoholic isn't in denial. He knows he has a problem. He denies it, possibly to avoid social reprimand, but inwardly, he is well aware that putting away a few cases of beer every week or a daily pint of whiskey is not normal. That river in Egypt? It's a dry bed—we know we are addicted, we just don't know what to do about it. And you don't think you *can* do anything about it. When you are at the peak of the addiction, envisioning a life without the offending substance is incomprehensible. Your body is sick, and your *mind* is diseased.

So over the years, I attempted to pull back, off and on. They call this strategy maintenance drinking. It doesn't last. It's a parry the demon plays with you for a while. It's more than happy to play the game because it wrote the rulebook. And it knows you will come back to the major leagues again. Usually, you're not even gone that long. I look back now and can see the plateaus to the addiction I stepped on over the years. The first one, I ascended in the language school in the military. Then the spring break vacation my freshman year of college. Another was after physical therapy school. Every plateau was a new playing field. Pullbacks or not, I can now clearly see the intake only increased with each upward step over the years. A simple, chart graph would show the line rising steadily over time along the grid. No one cried foul—the umpire of the game knows it is rigged. But I still had one more step to reach the summit before I would fall into a catastrophic descent.

After a break-up from a two and a half year relationship with a turbulent Californian girl, I had a sudden brainstorm with my new found release. I was on the phone with a friend from Indiana one late Saturday morning, beginning the usual nursing of a few bottles to warm up the weekend. He had recently gotten a divorce. In-between our usual bitching of the dark truths of the universe, Dave planted a grand idea in my head. To put in an application to work as a civilian therapist for the military—and head overseas. Far away from my recent social implosion. I had never thought of that as an option in my profession. I looked on the internet and, sure enough, there were plenty of jobs for physical therapists in the government. One of these prospects hailed from Germany.

Now it doesn't take an extended look into a shiny, crystal ball to see what will happen when you place a nicely progressing later stage alcoholic into the land where the natives not only invented the beer mug but perfected the use of it. Germans love to drink. There doesn't exist a coffee shop, cafe or restaurant where you can't get a beer. There are even vending machines that drop the can of hops for a euro and a half. The Germans, or Bavarians as I was in the southern region, drink all day long. The thick, wheat of Weizen or Bier with the one-inch foam head in the tall glasses is as much a staple to the Bavarian as the snack machine would be to us. And they use any excuse to consume it in mass quantities. Even on their day hikes through the country trails and lakes, beer gardens are set up along the routes. For in Germany, why exercise if you can't do it with the Weizen buzz? I have seen more than one gravestone of an American, long retired soldier or government worker, transferred out of this world early trying to keep up with the Bavarian lifestyle.

At the age of thirty-eight, I had one more ascent to climb to reach the pinnacle of my alcoholism. And I leaped on it full force when I landed in Deutschland, hitting the first Gastoff within hours of arriving. And I never left it the entire sixteen months I was there. Physical exercise had fallen by the wayside. In Hohenfels,

I got off work around 4:00 p.m. and headed directly to Michael's or Franz' establishment. These were places where the other Bavarians and American GS workers collected to drink. I tapped the Weizen until nine or ten o'clock and then took three or four bottles to my home up the hill. Michael himself commented once that I was an alcoholic. This statement is pretty significant when the observation comes from a German. The circling descent that began high above with my freshman year trip to D.C. was now in a free fall.

Physically, the addiction was beginning to raise its bloodshot eyes. I was periodically getting needles of pain in my right side in the mornings. This was the liver speaking, which began to complain of its extended overtime. My kidneys joined the block party with stabbings as well. The discomfort was matched by morning vertigo the first hour or two in the clinic after waking from the nightmares, accompanied by cottonmouth and a spike between my temples.

And I was at war with the military in Bavaria. The U.S. Army Medical Corps had utterly broken down, much like their civilian counterparts. The vision of military healthcare they portrayed during the telephone interview was nothing like the actual landscape revealed. The constant rage I had at the army didn't help the drinking. But I think no matter the circumstances, I would have been at Michael's or Franz' every night anyway. The alcoholic uses elation as equally as depression as reasons to stay close to his constant companion.

In November of 2007, I left the position in Hohenfels and worked briefly for a few months as a security contractor. In Kuwait. I had become so jaded with physical therapy and the corruption of healthcare in general that I favored working security in the boiling desert of the Middle East more than in a healthcare clinic back in the states. And I found that civilian security tied in with the military was just as incompetent and foul as the medical field within it. It was a foolish move, to begin with. I returned after only a few months and came back to California in complete and total despair.

Between April of 2008 and January of 2009 is where I crested the summit of the addiction. I was drinking over three cases of alcohol every week. Anytime I wasn't at work was spent with a bottle in my hand. Every morning was a recovery from the acute daily withdrawal. The disequilibrium had worsened the first few hours of every morning up and down the elevators to see my patients at the various hospitals. I was jittery and agitated all the time, and my blood pressure was well above normal ranges. The needles were more constant in my side and back, relieved only at night under the analgesic.

That Monday evening in August, as the room spun and my temples pounded, I stood at the peak, looking far below to the barren wastelands that had become my life. And I only wanted to sit down and die there, like a frozen Everest climber, and end it before the poison that flowed through me finally did in slow fashion. I knew cirrhosis of the liver would be arriving soon. Renal problems would follow. I saw it with patients in the hospital every day. And some of those addicts were close to my age. I knew what the body alerts were. Death had entered my neighborhood. And I didn't care. My soul was already deceased. The corporeal was only waiting to catch up finally.

I had reached the pinnacle that August. I stayed there for another five months. Alone on the summit, standing on the edge, with howling winds and bitter cold. Then on January 22nd, 2009, in an act of desperation . . . I finally jumped off.

SYNOPSIS

I write this first synopsis as a foreshadow of the rest of my method to beat alcoholism. I have, years after my last indulgence, told members of the Alcoholics Anonymous groups that I have gained complete and total recovery and not engaged in one of their "twelve steps." I've read *The Big Book* only as a thorough method of rejection due to their terrible outcomes.

Of course, their initial response is an alcoholic is never "cured." I attended exactly two meetings, eleven months after I put down the last beer can, simply to see what it was really about. I had a sneaking suspicion that I would see nothing but a negative and detrimental effect on those attempting to fight the addiction, by the participants sitting around in a room while they continuously rehashed their past over and over. When I entered their rooms, I was still in the long, two-year, protracted, neurochemical reprogramming of my recovery. Again, I state recovery and cure. When I stood up and stated my name, I then submitted I was beating alcoholism. The condescending looks and the reference to the old river in Egypt followed. They assumed I had quit it weeks ago. When I told the group it had been almost a year, there was only silence. This declaration was incomprehensible to them. It never occurred to the circle that one could stop without even starting their steps or getting a sponsor. They ignored me and quickly moved to the next person in the ring.

One of the seasoned sponsors came over as the group began to break up. He stated I probably wasn't a "true" alcoholic, to begin with. I believe the above chapter would show otherwise. Three cases of beer a week not only represents an alcoholic but reveals one who has perfected his craft. The rest of this book will show my journey of recovery, my *cure*. It will demonstrate how I beat the addiction in all its phases. I will also contrast the fact that for well over a decade, I have remained sober. Not one relapse, mind you. Compare this to AA's dismal results. I have found the formula to quit and be rid of this addiction. It doesn't involve a long, drawn-out process of "steps." There is no need for a guided sponsor. It is not an ongoing and never ending process. There is only one giant step the alcoholic needs to take.

And that is the end point of the synopsis. The last line of the chapter where I jumped off the pinnacle? It foreshadows the next chapter which reveals the one step an addict has to take to rid himself forever of the addiction. The addict simply has to quit.

CHAPTER 3

THE INFERNO

On January 22nd, 2009, somewhere after ten or eleven at night, I drank my last beer. I don't know why I picked the 22nd of that month. It wasn't a birthday or the beginning of a new year. There was no significance of the day whatsoever. I had been thinking about quitting since that prior August. I knew I was in serious trouble in the later stages of alcoholism. As that final night progressed, like every night, I was on my way to finishing a twelve pack. I emptied a can, grabbed another from the few remaining in the refrigerator. Halfway through it, a sudden tidal wave overtook me. I don't know where it came from; the piercing voice in my head.

Enough.

The morning of January 22nd began like every morning of my alcoholism. I had intermittent and restless sleep the night before of which I had grown accustomed. The processing and breakdown of the sugar from the intake tends to wake you up in the small hours. You keep a pitcher of ice water next to the nightstand for the impending cottonmouth. And you toss and turn in jittery, micro, night terrors as the tide of booze recedes from the body, leaving the rotting kelp of the daily withdrawal.

Large coffees and aspirin fuel the sluggish mornings as you wait for the transient vertigo to pass. I went through the day, turned in my paperwork from my home health patients in Turlock, California and resupplied my habit from the liquor store on the way home, popping the first can within minutes of arrival through the front door. And I began my usual indulgence of steady consumption.

But something happened that night. I began to re-evaluate. I was forty. I wasn't a Thai boxer anymore. Hell, I couldn't remember the last time I was in a gym. I wasn't on a cool military reconnaissance team. I was long past being a competitive bodybuilder. I was a good therapist—this was true. But I was a better alcoholic. *Alcoholic.* That was my master status now. I looked at a few recent photos of myself—my countenance was haggard and my eyes strained. I knew in five years or so, the medical problems would start to arrive. I would soon become the chronic patient in the hospital, not the one treating him.

How did I get here?

I remembered how I was normal once—long ago. At seventeen, I mostly didn't drink. I got along just fine in life without the beer. Now, I couldn't get along without it. I contemplated the long journey, where the storm had pulled me so far out to sea that I couldn't even see the shadows of the land any longer. The shoreline where ordinary people lived. Where people didn't wake up sick every morning. Every morning for me was comprised of illness. This lifestyle was insane. Three cases a week I drank. Three goddamn cases of beer. Forty years old. I would be dead at fifty.

Everyone dies. An unfortunate fact of life, numbed out by the white noise around us. But it is a fact—life is a temporary sublet whose lease isn't even guaranteed. But when one does die, he should be able to at least look back and observe a worthy existence. Whether the life was spent raising a family on a factory worker's wage or inventing Microsoft. What would I be able to claim when the Reaper opened the garage door and walked into my domain? I could, as of now, say I spent most of my adult life in an altered state of mind on God's creation because I couldn't put down the intoxicant. I could say I destroyed every fiber of my being, the precious gift given, because I had to have a beer can gripped in my fingers every minute I wasn't working. I could say my master status was an addict. I was an addict of beer. I was addicted to *beer.* Suddenly, it seemed incredibly stupid.

I kept sipping at it that night. But then I thought . . . what would life be like without it? What if I threw out the Dutch Uncle Buddy? It wasn't too late, after all. People did quit in their forties. People quit at sixty. The organs are extremely charitable and forgiving—if one ceases poisoning them. What if I could regain my life—where I spent my free time practicing martial arts and lifting weights again? To begin the pursuit of replacing the diseased body with a healthy one. And more importantly, curing the ill mind? There wasn't a rule, after all, that just because I drank heavily for thirteen years that I couldn't quit it. Nothing was set in stone. And the solution was simple. Stop.

I had a traumatized childhood. So had many others. Many of them became substance abusers. And a lot of them *didn't*. Why couldn't I be in the second category? Was it law that I must follow the path of dysfunction like my parents? Really, with my background, I shouldn't have even made it into the medical profession as a provider. But I did. I won the war. But I had gotten both legs blown off in the melee. And now it was time to fit a pair of prosthetics—and learn to walk again.

I threw the remaining beers in the trash. I went to the living room and sat down. I looked around at the various pictures on the walls. Many were remnants of all the places I had traveled, worked and lived. Photos and images all related to the alcohol that voyaged with them. My new life would be without it. I had just chucked it.

Ok, so now I'm not an alcoholic anymore. No problem, Jeeves.

I thought for a bit of what I knew of the twelve-step programs of recovery for various addictions. They pinpoint the thirty-day mark when they let you back into the world if you went to a rehabilitation center. Thirty days—where they say you have a small chance to stay sober. They tell you day one to look to the right and left of you. Those will be how many don't make it, they state boldly. So you walk into the "recovery" center, and the first thing out of their mouths is to inform you that you will probably fail to stay sober. Fantastic.

On top of that, they will tell you that you are a diseased addict and will be for life. That no matter what, you will always be sick. That you will always be in the process of recovery. When twenty years have passed, if you are one of the lucky ones, you will still be recovering. They tell you that you will never be well and whole. Then they begin their mantras of stating that the only way to recovery, which will never be complete, is their program, which they just told you most fail. Does anyone, besides me, see something slightly off with this grand philosophy?

I wasn't going to a rehab center. I wasn't even going to AA. It was a Thursday night when I emptied the last can of beer I would ever drink. I had looked up "acute alcohol withdrawal" on the search engines. All the sites, blogs and articles were in agreement. The first five days were the worst. The acute withdrawal could actually kill you, they said. I had only two home health patients scheduled for the next day. And only a few on Monday. This was the best scenario in which I could hope to go through the initial withdrawal.

It would start to hit as I came home Friday afternoon. Hopefully, the most catastrophic effects would have passed by Monday. And I only had a few hours on the road that day. I had once carried a hundred pounds for five miles on the SOT-A team with fifty below wind chills in Canada and remained out there for a few days in that deadly weather. I figured I could gut my way through a couple of hours of misery while I saw patients.

I would have to do this alone. There was zero chance that I would change my mind and check in somewhere. I knew all the doctors in the area as I was one of the primary home health therapists in the Turlock region. And I was a well-regarded practitioner. I couldn't foresee a few colleagues and the entire nursing staff knowing why I was there. I could see the rumors floating through the farmlands of the foothills: *Did you hear about that therapist? Yeah, Susie, from the cafeteria hospital saw him in a room while delivering trays. He's apparently a lush. Can you believe it? No, I had no idea either. . . .*

I'd rather it just take me altogether.

I know it was after 10 p.m. when I stopped drinking. I had happened to look at the clock on the oven as I pulled out my final can of hops. That I remember. I had already put away seven or eight, which now was only a moderate night. *Was I really going to do this?*

It had been quite a while since I had last attempted to quit. The last time I tried, I made it a day or two. And that was over a year ago. Even Kuwait had a black market for illegal booze. I thought about the remaining full ones in the trash basket. *Thirty days was the first milestone? I couldn't even imagine three days. A week was incomprehensible. How about the rest of my life? Not one beer the remainder of my days? This was a joke.*

I knew Hell was coming. It wasn't here yet; my diseased tissues hadn't gotten notice of my abrupt abstinence of the indulgence. But the package would be delivered soon via the Express Service, which would arrive on my doorstep tomorrow. I got up off the couch, walked to the bedroom and lifted the mattress. Under it was a loaded gun—.357 Magnum. It would do the job easily in one small click. Playtime was over.

Live sober or don't live at all.

I put the gun on the kitchen table. I would see it every day for the next thirty. One way or the other, I wasn't going to be an addict any longer. Then I went into my room and fell asleep.

The next morning, I awoke with the usual hangover. But not as intense as I had tossed the remaining soldiers into an early grave the prior night. Everything was normal as far as normal went for me. The sun rose in wild California, burning the fog away that rolled down the foothills into the Central Valley. I had a fitful night sleep, which I did every night, and didn't leave the apartment until 11 a.m. I only had a schedule of two patients out in the boondocks of the farmland that day. An eerie calm preceded the darkening storm clouds that were approaching as I left the small town of Gustine from my last patient and turned my paperwork in that early afternoon. The metaphor for what I knew was coming soon. It wouldn't be a gentle passing rainstorm. A typhoon was approaching.

It was strange going home to my apartment without first visiting the liquor store manager who was well acquainted with me. I wonder how many clerks in those stores over the years shook their heads as I left with copious amounts of beer under my arm every day? I paced around on my carpet. What exactly was I going to do for the next eight hours without the company of my Dutch Uncle? I looked at my small collection of movie DVDs and Netflix sitting on my table. So this was what sobriety was like? Boring.

The boredom soon passed. By late evening, an intense agitation had set in. And unbelievable cravings. Thirty days was the first major mark? I didn't think I would make it through the next thirty minutes. It had arrived—the beginning of acute alcoholic withdrawal. The first phase to recovery. I went out to the supermarket and bought gallons of Gatorade and teas to get me through. And a few quarts of ice cream. I had always heard that the rapid infusion of sugar from ice cream helps with the cravings. Then I returned home, noting all of the bars and lounges that I had passed. Just looking at the neon signs made my mouth water. It wasn't a distant forecast any longer. The tsunami was in sight, about a mile out to sea.

I slept only in small segments that night and awoke with severe anxiety. I sipped coffee the next morning and paced, staring vacantly. By the afternoon, I was in full withdrawal. I had tremors in my hands. Full-scale panic attacks rolled over and swept me away. I alternated between lying in bed, as the sweat began to flow, and sitting in the corner of the living room. The needles in my liver and kidneys had metamorphosed into small knives that dug and twisted, whether I moved or remained still. The curtain pulled back and revealed the illusion. This was my body for real without the induced amnesia.

By the evening, I was nearing the forty-eight-hour mark. I focused on each minute passing. Soon fifteen or twenty did. It was incremental agony—huddled in the familiar corner with my head in my hands, rocking back and forth. Then back to pacing the carpet. I picked up the gun on the table more than once.

Others have made it through this, so can you. Sure, there were people right now all over the world who suddenly stepped through the doors that held them in their addiction. And they were sitting in rehab centers with anti-anxiety medication while the blizzard whirled around the walls. But then again, the price they would pay would probably be repeated visits—if they ever beat their addictions at all. And right now they were being informed the likelihood was they wouldn't.

I was solo in the apartment with no help. I hadn't even told anyone what I was doing. But I had done the only thing that an addict can do if he genuinely wants to relieve himself of that title. I had made the mental affirmation that it was over. I was in Hell for sure. And I would have been in the same inferno locked away somewhere. The fires would cool in due time. I didn't need mantras or steps to a program. One thing is needed for the addict—the refusal of the offending substance ever again. All the references stated I would feel better in five days from the last swallow. I hadn't even completed two yet.

The demon didn't whisper anymore. It roared. It beckoned me to end the internal fury with a ten minute trip to the liquor store. *All you have to do is pop the tab, and in a half-hour, you'll feel fine again,* it said. *Do you really want to go through this? We all have to die anyway . . . let me at least take you with a comfortable buzz.*

No.

I kept looking at the clock to the forty-eight-hour mark. The knives in my side and back continued to twist. I sweated and shook. But I wasn't dead yet. I made two days. I could make another two. Then it was almost over. The dust would settle from the ground blast I had just ignited. How long were five days? One hundred and twenty hours. Just like a military short timer's countdown, I would take it hour by hour. As I curled into a fetal position on the bed and tried to sleep it away, I knew I had seventy-two of those hours left. Seventy-two and I exit the acute withdrawal phase. If my heart didn't cease first.

Horrid nightmares descended during the tossing and brief intermittent periods of sleep. At 3:00 a.m., I awoke, convinced the walls were closing in on me. Night terror shortened my breath as my heart raced. During the small hours of day three, I thought I had died and gone to Hell. Lying in the damp sheets, I recalled the past. Ex reconnaissance soldier on the tough SOT-A teams. Former Thai boxer. I didn't feel so tough now, curled in a mixture of sweat and tears. And all the pretty birds had gone south this winter. I was completely alone. The demon finally removed its long-worn mask. The countenance had looked pleasant enough all of these years under intoxication. But now I saw its true face—reflected in my mirror. The hideous monster that wanted my body and soul. And I was wrestling it now as the claws tore deep, trying to hang on to me. The badass loan shark had arrived to collect the interest on its due.

Sunday passed in a haze. I barely ate anything, feeling nauseous as soon as I swallowed the minute amounts of food. I hadn't slept more than an hour straight through during the past few days. I couldn't even sit to watch a movie. I spent most of the afternoon staring at the wall. I kept a journal of the process. My shaking hand scribbled the symptoms as they came. So years later if I ever felt the need to drink again, all I had to do was reread the nightmare. The words that have now made it to this book. It still makes me shudder when I look at them.

Monday, on day four, I went to work to see the few patients I had on my list. I hadn't been outside since Friday evening when I stocked the refrigerator. I got into my car and immediately erupted with hyperactive anxiety. I forced myself to breathe deep and slow. I kept it together by sheer force of will at the first patient's house and then drove a few blocks to the gas station for a large coffee while another anxiety attack hit me. An hour later, I went to the next house, a town away, and repeated the entire process. *One more day and it will be better. This nightmare isn't forever. Just keep walking through the gauntlet. Every member of the tribe is pummeling you, but the end is in sight. Just keep charging, hour by hour.*

I waited until after five in the early evening to turn in my paperwork as I wished to speak to pretty much no one at the office. I passed the time, after seeing my couple of patients, by sitting in a coffee shop, watching others come and go. *Look at me, everyone. You don't know it, but the guy with his home health bag next to him is in alcoholic withdrawal. It's a real blast, folks. If you stay for that free refill, you might actually witness his heart bursting through his chest.*

There was one nurse left at the office when I arrived. I mumbled greetings, put my notes together and filed them, trying to scurry out as fast as I could. She caught a glimpse at my face and stared intently.

"You alright? You look awful," she noted.

"Yeah, I know." I wanted to get the hell out of there. I had never hidden the fact that I drank like a moderate size school of young guppies. And I had mentioned a few weeks earlier that I was thinking about disowning my Dutch Uncle for good. RNs aren't known for having much slip past them.

"Oh my God. Did you . . . stop drinking?"

"Yeah." Christ, I felt terrible.

"How long?" She already had the blood pressure cuff and stethoscope out and ready.

"I'm on day four."

"You're in *acute withdrawal*? By *yourself* ?" The cuff was around my arm. My pulse was close to a hundred beats a minute, and my blood pressure stood at 160/104. These readings are definitely not indicative of a good state of affairs unless you're an impending stroke.

"We need to check you in." *Oh, hell no. I'd rather die . . . thanks anyway.* I argued with her for about ten minutes before she gave up. Having another health practitioner this concerned didn't exactly elevate my spirits. I didn't go to the hospital. I went home and consumed a large bowl of ice cream instead. The evening became night, and the night passed once again with only small, episodic bouts of nightmare ridden sleep.

Almost as if on cue to the hour did the initial withdrawal symptoms begin to abate. On Tuesday, I went to work with the few patients I had on the schedule. Again, I drank coffee in-between each house visit. But the intermissions of panic weren't as long or intense. A severe flu still would have been more fun, but I was getting through. And that night, at the long-awaited one hundred and twenty-hour mark, my system had calmed somewhat. My hands weren't shaking, and I didn't sweat now. I could actually sit still for fifteen minutes. I didn't feel great, but it was superb to what I had just gone through. It had been a long five days. And I was through it at the other end.

After the initial cliff dive into the fire lake, you emerge covered in the volcanic ash, still unable to recognize yourself. You're not boiling anymore but still remain in the dark caverns of Hades with no idea how to find your way out. And I only had a few guide maps to the exits and air-conditioned rooms above.

I had bought several books on alcoholism and was reading my own biography in them as I went through the pages. At least I wasn't the only one, it seemed. The difference was the other newly reformed were locked away with a fully trained staff during their withdrawal, and I was alone in an apartment. And every book repeated the mantra. *Rehab, then go to AA, get a sponsor, and start the twelve steps. You're an addict. You'll always be an addict. You'll always be sick. You can't beat alcoholism without AA. This is the only way.*

Well, I had only been sober for five days, so maybe I couldn't talk yet. But I *did* make it through. I *didn't* give in to the cravings. I hadn't given myself a choice. My new contract stated that I and Jack London's John Barleycorn were done—no negotiation. I wasn't at the thirty-day mark though. And the cherished six-month crossing was incomprehensible. I still couldn't imagine a life without alcohol. But I had just come out of the inferno. And I wasn't going through *that* again, that was for sure. I didn't think about life without alcohol or the next six months. I made thirty days clean the next goal. It seemed like two incarnations away.

I had been sober for five days. I had no idea what I would feel like at day thirty. But I would soon. I had just thrust a sword into the demon and now waited for it to bleed out. I went to sleep that Tuesday night and mentally prepared for the next phase that would lead to my recovery and cure.

SYNOPSIS: PHASE ONE—ACUTE WITHDRAWAL

There is no easy way to get through the acute withdrawal phase, which is the first five days of sobriety. Depending on the level of addiction, medical intervention may be needed. I chose to do it alone and full disclosure: *this was probably foolish and dangerous.*

The first five days are going to be a nightmare—no matter how or where you do it. The night sweats and terrors will be there, even if you're locked away in your bunk in rehab. If you're a very light alcoholic, the three-to-four-drink-a-night type, then you aren't going to nearly go through all of this internal drama. You'll probably only be irritable for a few months like the very light ex-smokers when they dust off the last ash and then have only periodic cravings. My above scenario is for us solid professionals. Those of us who consumed three cases of barley or the equivalent a week.

My own experience of the first five days seems to be accurate for most of us who quit. I managed to keep a journal during my entire recovery, which is now complete. The first few pages are broken sentences, keywords and the rants of someone who is practically hysterical with mental and physical anguish. There is a reason I state you are attempting to walk out of an inferno.

I would have no problem with someone who chose to go to a rehab center to wait out the first thirty days if it wasn't such a program of indoctrination. And that's mentally dangerous as they are grabbing the addict at their absolute weakest—like the cults who target those from dysfunctional homes. Think about what the first thing they say is; that the person to the left and right of you will fail and go back to substance abuse. That sixty-six percent of everyone who enters the doors are not going to stay sober. How exactly is that supposed to be endearing to a successful mindset? Then they start the mantras, setting one up for a life, if the person even makes the thirty-three percent, to be addicted to AA for the rest of their existences. It is important to note that many researchers think a thirty-three percent rate of success for traditional twelve-step programs is a gracious prophecy at best. No matter who is doing the numbers, even AA clearly states that you have a higher chance of failure than success. How this has not led someone to change their protocols is beyond me. If someone did choose the thirty day rehab center, then my advice is to get through the acute withdrawal and immediate post-acute effects and then walk out the door. If they ask why, tell them a thirty-three percent chance of success doesn't exactly fill you with confidence for their protocols.

My strategy for the first five days was to focus only on those initial 120 hours of sobriety. Nothing else was on the table. Trying to think of day thirty is incomprehensible, let alone the rest of your life as the acute withdrawal sets in. The only deal with yourself is to get through 120 hours. And you take that hour by hour. If you, by some chance, can sleep at all, then that's a few hours knocked off. Even an hour of watching television is an hour gone.

I broke every day down into sections. I woke and thought about getting to noon. Then 6:00 p.m. Then to 10:00 p.m. where I would attempt to drift off into sleep. Then get through the night. You only have to go through this five times, and you're out of the acute phase.

I kept high concentrations of juices, water and ice cream in the refrigerator. I attempted to watch DVDs but couldn't sit still more than a few minutes. Trying to read a book was ludicrous.

Mainly, you just get through 120 hours. You make a list of 120 then start checking them off. You have to use small goals. Break 100 hours. Then 80. All the way down to zero. Then at 120 hours completed, it is almost like magic. You aren't going to feel great—but you'll never again feel like the hell you just went through.

And remember the feeling. This is where you cement the contract with yourself. An unshakeable deal. A *no exceptions* oath is taken. The raised hand and swearing on the universe that you will never make yourself feel this way again. I don't think one needs any more steps than this one. The one-step is to simply quit it with an understanding that there is never going to be a time to test the waters again. That you will never see if "this time, I can just drink socially." You can become cured, but you will still have the old chemistry of an addict. AA is partly right about this matter. But once you get through the acute phase, you look at alcohol like it is arsenic. You promise yourself that you're never going to walk through this again. For you have begun the journey of a now newly sober person.

CHAPTER 4

ASCENT

The physical misery of the acute withdrawal had passed by the morning of the sixth day from the abrupt cessation of the liquid barley. It was a unique experience to not wake up with vertigo for the first few hours of the day for a change. Or a raging headache and queasy stomach. There were still stabbings of pain in my liver and kidney area, but the intensity had lessened somewhat and would continue to decrease over the next few months until they finally would disappear altogether. The morning seemed like morning, sunshine and rays breaking up the mist in the California Central Valley's mild version of winter. The air was fresh and cool as I stepped out to begin my rounds in home health. My caseload was picking up again to regular eight hour days. Had I really gone almost a week without opening a beer? It was a foreign land. The last five days seemed like a blurred haze by that Wednesday morning. A nightmare that I had awakened from, whose blackness receded like the early morning fog on the foothills in the distance. Of course, I felt different, even in just five days—the poison was out of my system now. A novel cognizance glided over me.

This was what it was like not to feel sick every day.

Normality. Just waking up from sleep, even if intermittent, instead of waking up from an induced coma. The difference between falling asleep versus passing out. The acute withdrawal hadn't killed me after all. And now it was over.

Now the emotional frenzy would begin—a five ringed circus with chaotic, angry clowns who would run along the perimeter in my head. They would continue to the next landmark—thirty days. The short hop to when those in rehab centers would be released back into the world. There was a reason they kept newly sober candidates in these places until day thirty.

The acute withdrawal, the first stage of recovery, is the worst and the shortest. Then begins the long, protracted withdrawal. The books I had read on the subject stated it would extend eighteen to twenty-four months. The time it would take for the brain and neurochemistry to rebalance itself. The amount required before natural opiates would learn to drop by their own accord without the aid of the intoxicant. Whereat two years you look in the mirror and finally can say you're recovered. The milestone where you can tell yourself you're not an addict any longer.

The landmarks in-between are thirty days, six months and finally, when you shake the biting dog completely off at two years. This timeline to recovery is another point where I break from the AA philosophy. AA recognizes that the second year of recovery is a lot like the first. But AA states the recovery is ongoing for the rest of your life. I'm telling the addict that the two-year mark is when he can say he's cured.

After the initial melee of acute withdrawal, the cravings hit and settle, driving their stakes into the ground. During the first five days, you have cravings as well but are so sick that they are largely secondary. Now they intensify tenfold and last for hours at a time. And they are going to hit whether you are sitting in a recovery center or flopped in front of your Netflix. *The only way to deal with cravings is to ignore them.* How can it be that simple, the pundits cry? Because it is.

There is no trick that will keep cravings away. They will come, turn the corner and run you over like a freight train, and then they pass. In the beginning, they are almost constant. That first month after the acute phase, pretty much all the newly sober will think about is alcohol. It won't be that way forever. I'm now well past a decade of sobriety and the cravings still periodically emerge. But today, they are much less intense and vaporize quickly, struggling breaths of a buried demon trying to resurrect his life. And they are very infrequent now. Every once in a while, I have an intense one—not often, but it still happens. But I've had so many and have defeated so many of them that I know they will move on, usually in a few hours. I let them slide like a wave that rolls over me but then passes toward the shoreline.

The steepest barrier to recovery, however, in the initial stages, is the intense cravings that are nonstop. That's when the recovering addict is in the most danger. An alcoholic who has just quit has about a billion neural memories of nothing but drinking. And suddenly, he realizes in new sobriety that he is surrounded by visual social triggers wherever he looks. It isn't apparent until after you put the bottle down. Things would be a lot easier for the newly sober if they were all placed on their own island and had nothing but coconut milk to pour down the gullet. But the rest of the world doesn't cater to the recent abstinence. The newly sober have to live in this world. A lot of people don't have the luxury of being able to take thirty days to hang out in rehab, locked away from the rest of the planet. Most have to deal with the initial intense cravings while they continue to exist on the terrain where they once drank.

You walk outside, and a million billboard signs bombard you with beer and wine. Neon lights blink from corner bars on every block. You retreat home and turn on the television, and what do you see? Steelworkers after their shift in an advertisement with frosty mugs. It makes you salivate at the beginning of the recovery process. I distinctly remember going to an after-work get-together at my eleventh day of sobriety. We were at a restaurant lounge. I sat next to my coworkers with a coffee cup much to their raised eyebrows as prior I usually held a thirty-two-ounce mug. I remember staring at the bar counter. Ice cold glasses pulled from the freezer, causing the perfect one-inch foam to form on top of the golden wheat. I practically snapped the coffee cup handle. Eleven days was entirely too early to participate in an event like this. But I made it through. When I returned home, the craving passed—briefly.

There is a reason that so many hide in "the rooms" in AA, I believe. To escape from the social triggers that induce cravings. And this would probably not be a bad idea in the first six months. A recent former addict should probably avoid all social contact during this time. For the reason that most after work adult contact involves alcohol. I could even see attending a program like AA every night during the initial phases of recovery. It wouldn't hurt to hear everyone else's "story." And grasp the understanding that indeed, the tale is the same. But I can't recommend their program, even in the initial stages of recovery, because of a world view that the other members will force upon the newly sober.

The contention I hold is; first, most of them fail sobriety using the twelve-step program. The program they indoctrinate into the newly sober that first month, whether in AA or the twelve-step based rehab center. And second, the successful ones never regain their lives. They are twenty years sober and still going to AA every night. Every meeting, they are still regurgitating their "story." They state AA teaches you how to live with sobriety. Live? They are trapped in meetings the rest of their lives. They aren't living; they are imprisoned. The minority who do stay sober are terrified to live on their own. They don't have an alcohol problem any longer. Now they have a psyche problem. So yes, I'm pointing people away from the AA philosophy completely in all phases of recovery.

The simple fact is the recovered alcoholic will always have periodic cravings whether he sits in the meeting house or not. And the first month, those cravings are ungodly intense and almost continuous. And there is only one way to beat the craving. It is very simple. I don't need twelve steps to chant or a sponsor. I don't need *The Big Book* on my shelf. There is a simple key to staying sober when the cravings come. Once again, I say: *You ignore them until they go away.*

Willpower. Either you are going to develop it or you won't. It apparently isn't created in AA as most fail their program. With all the protocols, steps, sponsors and mantras, most in AA don't develop the willpower to stay sober. They do not succeed with sobriety. And a lot of them fail in that first month. Most go back to drinking. So how are they going to rationalize to me that their program works? They will cry that it helps some. Sure. The minority that stays sober is now trapped forever in their "rooms." But most do not succeed. If AA were a business, they would be out of business. You cannot claim successful standard operating procedures when most are not successful. Period.

This formula given by the twelve steppers, after acute withdrawal, will set the stage for how an AA person will conduct his life, once indoctrinated into their methods of sobriety. The counselors give them the same formula in the recovery center. Either they are in AA after the acute phase, or they are in the rehab building, preparing themselves for AA with the same group meetings, same protocols and same mantras. *The Big Book* sits on the shelves at the treatment centers too. A new candidate comes out of the initial withdrawal stage surrounded by the sages who tell him the AA protocol is the only way. Then they hand him *The Big Book*, which reinforces the fact.

He'll get a sponsor who will indoctrinate the mantra as well. The sponsor will become obsessed with "the twelve steps." They are continually harping on what step the protégé is on. Everyone rambles on about the steps. One day they are on step three. Then they get to step six. Then they fall backward to step four. "Work the program, work the steps," the sponsor says. The newly sober may think a great deal of this is bunk. But if he voices this opinion, an avalanched chorus will crash on his head from the other members. *De-Nile—that river in Egypt.* How clever. Little side note, AA—when you continue to chant a mantra over and over— you're not a helpful group any longer. You're a cult.

I have a serious problem with the steps, first of all. Not all of them, but the synopsis of that checklist is a recipe for failure. The very first one states the alcoholic is powerless over alcohol. That's ridiculous. This initial mantra is the premise that will eternally cast the addict into the victimhood mindset that he is forever diseased.

After my acute withdrawal ended, I developed a much different view before thirty days elapsed. And that mindset is you have total power over alcohol. There may be something to the genetic predisposition to drink. Or it may be socially learned as some experts believe. Anyone with alcoholic family members is more prone to have problems. But the power, like the power of everything in a person's life, lies with the person. You don't go to the liquor store. If you're drinking too much, you stop. Last I heard, it isn't essential that a person's diet includes alcohol. That first step should be replaced with the mental contract that you will not touch the offending substance again. If the addict states this out loud then follows the declaration, no matter what happens, he won't be an addict much longer. Of course, if he drinks again, he'll be an addict again most likely. So you don't chance it, don't risk it and don't jeopardize the new sobriety. You follow the contract. You actually decide this on day one of sobriety as I stated in the last chapter. But it is that first month after acute withdrawal where the oath will face its greatest test.

In the second phase of recovery, you cement even further in your mind that you will follow the contract you made in the acute withdrawal. You follow it if you lose your job. You follow the contract if you lose half your assets in the stock market. You follow it if you get divorced. If your best friend dies or your damn dog gets run over by a truck. No exceptions. You make the contract solid in your newly clear mind, and you follow it. That's it, and that's all.

Believing in a power greater than ourselves that can restore us to sanity isn't a terrible second step. But there exists another great adage. *God helps those who help themselves.* And what if you're an atheist addict? I guess they are just out of luck, according to AA. AA believes you can only succeed with the steps and the second one the atheist can't follow. That helps that particular group, not at all. I believe in a God but also consider that a great deal of the time we are on our own, out here in the badlands of humanity. The second step would do exactly squat for me. And the third step of turning our lives over to Him in that manner largely follows the second step. Again, too bad for the atheists and bottoms up, I guess.

The AA philosophy, initiated in the first month, is preparing the newly sober to be professional victims who are helpless to their addiction. During the second phase, I am telling you to develop a resolute mindset. One where you will gain fortitude and will. If you can gain that, you will build the wall that will keep the enemy out of your new fortress.

Steps four through seven are all an extension of two and three. Four includes making the moral inventory of ourselves. I think we got that when we quit drinking. As far as all the stupid things we did when drunk, they are all the same things that everyone does when they are drunk. I worked at more than one bar and nightclub as security and as a bartender. The stories and the drama are all identical. It is a plethora of stupid witticisms, casual sex, chaos, and possibly a few nights in jail. Alcohol alters the mind. A person will do foolish things when the mind is altered.

The alcoholic writes ridiculous emails to people when he's drunk. He calls an old flame at the peak of intoxication and makes an idiot of himself. Or one fine day in Bavaria, he staggers back to his house in mid-afternoon and falls on his face right in front of the neighborhood. I had a bruise on my forehead for a week for that one. Is it essential that I have a moral inventory of my alcoholic past? Or should I chalk it up to "dumb things I did when drunk?" And you don't need to confess this to the other sages to reinforce what we already know as step five states we should. I can easily explain it: a drunk and moronic behavior is the same thing. As an ex-Catholic, I never bought into that some collared priest had this holy power to absolve one of his sins. There is one entity who can do that. If you need to confess, then you can do it to Him. If you're an atheist, then you don't. But generally, the stupid behavior ceases when the person stops gulping from the bottle.

Steps six and seven once again call to God to remove the defects. God doesn't need to remove anything. You remove the defect by following the contract you made to never touch alcohol for the rest of your days. Again, see the old adage of

God helping those who help themselves. And again, AA is telling you, in the second phase of recovery, the higher power will be the answer. I'm telling you to develop your will and realize it is you who has the power to stay sober.

Step eight, I agree with to a point. If you grievously wronged someone, you should make amends whether you are an alcoholic or not. But then AA takes it to the point where they want the recovering addict to go around and find every single person he slighted in any way at all and practically fall on his newly sober knees. It comes to the effect where the person makes a spectacle of himself. Steps nine through eleven are more of the preceding steps.

I'll take step twelve. A spiritual awakening with a message to others. And I am using a message to help others. I'm stating out loud do not get involved in AA for the long term if you want sobriety. I'm exposing the rampant failure of the program and philosophy. I'm showing a better way—from one who has remained sober for over ten years.

But the newly sober, after the acute withdrawal, immediately becomes indoctrinated. He works the program. He never stops working the program. He has the mantra memorized by thirty days. Later down the line, he becomes a sponsor. He joins AA committees. He helps organize national events. He now centers everything in his life around AA. Of course, they told him his entire life should focus on nothing but recovery. A recovery that never ends. He is always in recovery. His whole life outside of work is AA. He doesn't go on vacation unless he can get access to the rooms. Wherever he travels, he knows where the meeting house is. Because for him, it is essential that he sits in the rooms and reminds himself how terrible his life once was in the prior addiction. He becomes distanced from his spouse. She wasn't an alcoholic so isn't a part of AA. The marriage becomes strained. Doesn't she understand that everything must revolve around his recovery? Even if it has been ten years since his last drink. She realizes she is not part of his life—his new mistress is AA. They end up divorced. And that's ok for him. It works for him because they brainwash in the first month that he must sacrifice all for his unending recovery.

Does this sound like a healthy way to live?

My indoctrination is a bit different for the second phase. As I stated, the cravings are persistent and intense in the beginning as you step out of the acute phase. You will be feeling just grand, say, at day twenty-five, and you're riding down the block and suddenly see a billboard with a man holding the foamed haired demon. The force of the craving lifts you out of your car seat. The battle begins in the chambers of the mind: the demon screams to hit the liquor store. And you ignore it. The day you quit, you will walk through the acute withdrawal phase. But remember—that first day of sobriety you put in your mind that you *will never touch alcohol again*. And then when the acute phase ends, you reiterate the fact over and over. You don't let your mind negotiate—try to lull you into thinking this time you will be a moderate drinker.

There is no point in having this internal debate. You know you aren't a moderate drinker. You *were* an alcoholic. You don't have to remain an alcoholic, contrary to the AA mantra, but if you pick up the bottle, you will be again. You've developed an addiction, whether genetic or socially learned isn't relevant. It's like smoking—if you start again, you will regress to the same number of daily cigarettes you sucked away before you quit. If you smoked a lot before you quit, then once you start again, you will smoke just as many. That's how addiction works. The only way to beat the smoking addiction is not to smoke—ever. The only way to overcome the alcoholic addiction is never to drink again. You already put in your mind the day you quit that you will never pick up the bottle. And you reiterate to yourself in the second phase to follow this oath until your last breath on earth.

And after a while, even in the second phase, you will realize that you can beat the cravings. The more you conquer their impending force, the stronger you become. Because you know they are going to fade. The craving hits, you ride it out. Then it subsides. When it hits again, you know you can ignore it. You know it will retreat. You just have to wait it through. Every time.

The mind is the most powerful weapon you have. If you tell yourself there is *no negotiation*, that you will never taste the offending substance again, the neurons will act accordingly. And as time passes, the intensity and frequency of the cravings decrease. It will be better by day thirty than it was on day six. But when an unusually intense one sweeps you away, you ride the wave until it subsides. You can do that because you have been there before. This is the fortitude of mental will that you build in the second phase of recovery.

This building of mindset is what the second phase should resemble. There *should* be a safe haven to go to, not only the first thirty days but first six months or so. *Especially* during that initial thirty days when the cravings are the strongest and constant. Also, so the person can be educated about the nature of the addiction. There should be a safe house where he can sit without being surrounded by the social triggers that intensely induce the cravings, which will be bad enough that first month. There is nothing wrong with a support group during the initial phases. But then the person should start to wean off of it and return to his life—a now sober life. But AA won't give you that. They offer a mental prison instead.

In a program that I would set up, the newly sober would go to a meeting every night. Then he would eventually downgrade to three times a week. Then once a week. Then, two years later, as the cravings are now only periodic, the person can return to a more normal existence. And continue until he can finally look at himself in the mirror and recognize a *former* alcoholic. For now, he is cured. Unfortunately, that safe haven I describe doesn't exist in most rehab settings. There is usually only AA.

For the pundits at AA, the above statement of cure is heresy. They state there is never a cure. The person cannot be cured. He is an alcoholic. He is always an alcoholic. He is diseased. He will always be diseased. Recovery never ends. An alcoholic is always recovering.

Well, here's my answer: *When you have a program where the majority succeed, then you can talk.* You don't, AA. So please sit down and be quiet. I'm not interested in why you fail—your endless reasons and excuses backed by your nonstop chants and mantras. Your rates of success with the twelve steps are dismal at best. Most don't complete the steps. Most trip and fall flat on their faces. They fail. I am in the second decade of an alcohol-free life. Maybe you might want to look at how I did it.

There was a sequence to my complete recovery. At which two years, I began to state I was once an alcoholic but was now cured. The first five days of acute withdrawal ended that Tuesday night. The first landmark. At that time, it was still incomprehensible that I would remain sober for the rest of my existence. But I had survived the worst experience I had ever gone through in my life. I would make the rest comprehensible for certain. Because during the second phase, I told myself it was over. I reiterated to myself many times a day that I would never touch alcohol again. My next milepost would be thirty days. It wasn't a matter of *if* I would cross thirty days. I resolved in my head that it was an absolute that I was going to pass this point. And whatever happened in-between happened. Because I had told my mind I was through with alcohol forever.

Thirty days is when they release you from the rehab center and send you to AA to begin the continuous recovery, which would never end. And I did need recovery as well. I shattered my body and soul with alcoholism. It didn't mean they had to stay broken. *You will always be diseased? Forever an alcoholic?* No. I refused to accept that guideline from their precious books I had read. I would recover. I knew at day six that I was not going to go down the road of endless recovery that had everything but the end. I would find the cure.

At day six, I could not imagine day thirty. A month of living sober? I could safely say that a month hadn't gone by without alcohol since that graduation night at eighteen. Thirty days? My mouth was watering for the cool wheat at day six. So I just concentrated on making it to day seven. One week. Then I would work on getting to two. Double that, and I would almost be at the next milepost. I broke the thirty days down into small, segmental goals just like I broke the initial five days down into segmental goals. Except in phase two, my goals were comprised of days passed instead of mere hours.

During the initial five days of acute withdrawal, I hadn't eaten much. I knew my body, right down to the cellular level, would be going into repair mode. Another problem with twelve steppers is they never consider healthy living once they step into the rooms. They spend every night drinking cup after cup of coffee, gobbling sugar goodies into their system to counter the cravings while sucking one cigarette after another. And I used sugar as well in the second phase. Ice cream and large chocolate milkshakes from McDonald's. These additives decreased with time as the frequency of cravings lessened. But that first few weeks, the counter at McD's knew me by name. Today, I still keep a quart of ice cream in the freezer. But it takes a lot longer to finish it now. And it has nothing to do with cravings anymore. You may need these "bad foods" to get you through the second phase. But unlike AA, I am not going to endorse this lifestyle forever.

While the body is repairing itself, it is essential to give it an infusion of healthy nutrients to aid in its recovery. This tactic is especially important in those first thirty days. Now, I'm not going to tell you that you can just have a swell diet and bypass the gauntlet. A lot of the holistic program that I will give will fall into place weeks to months later. I *started* a healthy diet and slowly made it better as the cravings began to fade. The first thing I did was to eliminate most fast foods to maybe once a week. Then I developed a vegetable and fruit rich intake. I added this to an influx of daily protein in the form of chicken and various fish. Whole grains, instead of processed food, were my new sources of energy. Different varieties of rice became a constant staple. Very much like my diet when I was a competitive bodybuilder in my early twenties.

I didn't eliminate coffee altogether but kept it at four cups at most a day. I did use nicotine like everyone in the rooms does. On the one hand, nicotine and sugar actually can relieve cravings, but chronic use can induce cravings later on. If you can get through the initial phases without cigarettes, that is a plus for sure. But the only thing I focused on was day thirty. You have to understand that constant sugar and nicotine use cause fluctuations in the body's chemistry, which affects mood. Those substances induce anxiety long term. And what did the brain memory use to relieve anxiety just a week ago? Alcohol. Anxiety induces even more cravings. So I kept the substances that elevate anxiety to a minimum once I broke past thirty days. During the first thirty days, you are just trying to survive. You could have a perfect diet, and it isn't going to diminish the cravings the first month.

I can understand the person using whatever he needs to in the first month, to month and a half to get through. I sure did. The greatest risk to failure in sobriety is in that first month or so—whether in AA or not. But eventually, the healthy lifestyle diet should substitute any offending additives once things begin to subside. Carolyn Knapp, author of *Drinking: A Love Affair*, was successful in staying sober. But then AA became her life. And in AA she never adopted a healthy recovery, smoking incessantly, well past her last drink. She died in her seventh year into sobriety—lung cancer. And she spent that seven years obsessed with recovery. She wrote about recovery, but the fact is she, like all members in AA, died imprisoned by it.

The newly sober should *start* to implement a healthy diet as soon as acute withdrawal concludes. It will make the next month easier—as easy as it can be. I knew that I was going to have to recreate everything about myself. But first, I had to get through the next month. The physical hell was over. Now I entered the mental hell. On top of the cravings, an emotional roller coaster began after day six.

I reread, years later, the fading pages in the journals of 2009. The memoir of a man slowly climbing up the switchbacks, trying to ascend out of Dante's sphere. I battled the cerebral inferno every single night. My gym membership remained unused as I had severe insomnia and was exhausted most of the time. And when I did sleep for two hours or so, the time was filled with horrific nightmares. I came home from work drained, knowing I would battle cravings for the next six to seven hours before I would attempt to sleep again, marking another day completed into the journey before I lay down. I had the entire series of *The Sopranos* to keep me occupied but could only sit for ten minutes at a time. It would take me two hours to get through a forty-five-minute episode.

It was still incomprehensible to think about the rest of my life without alcohol. So I kept the goals in my head. The next milestone would be at thirty days. Then six months. They say at six months you have a decent chance, as most don't make it that far in AA. If I could make one month, then surely I could repeat the process five more times—especially if the trail became easier as the months passed. But I largely didn't contemplate six months or the rest of my life. I kept my focus on getting to day thirty.

I took long breaks between my patients so I would arrive home later. The less time I was idle, the better, I imagined. I mentally made checkmarks to get through the day. The real danger was after work, though. It was difficult to get through the six or seven hours until I went to bed. But every day I did it without going to the liquor store, I became a little stronger. *I didn't drink yesterday, so I can do it again today.*

My days in the beginning of protracted withdrawal went as follows. It will be the same for anyone new to sobriety. There is no getting around this roller coaster just like there isn't any way to avoid the acute withdrawal, no matter where you decide to do it.

I would wake up feeling exhausted from insomnia. Every night I would try to go to sleep around 11 p.m. and would lie awake for several hours. Finally, I would drift off into horrid dreams only to wake up again at five in the morning. Then I would lie around, tossing and turning, until I could begin to drift into a half-sleep, and then the alarm would go off.

I would go to work, seeing bar neons, billboards; everything constantly reminding me of my new sobriety. My mouth watered daily for alcohol. But it was much worse when I got home between five or six in the evening. I was too tired to go to the gym but too hyperactively anxious to go to bed early. And it wouldn't matter if I went to bed early because I would wake up in two hours—as if the mind would only allow the minimal rest needed. So I would sit in the apartment. Watch fifteen minutes of *The Sopranos* then get up and pace around. I would try to read a book and usually last about two pages. Cravings would come, hit hard for an hour, subside and come back thirty minutes later. I concentrated on getting to nine o'clock and then making it to 11 p.m. At 11 p.m., I slashed a tic mark on my piece of paper for days in sobriety.

The super intense cravings in the first month or so are only part of the initial ordeal of the protracted withdrawal. The emotional upheaval will be as intense as the mouth-watering for the bottle. It is going to be miserable. One hour you feel euphoric as the birds chirp outside. An hour later you feel suicidal, cast into a black abyss of depression. Panic attacks are daily, the walls themselves seem to close in when they strike. And anxiety is chronic. The recent addict has just informed the brain that it intends to continue without the assumed intoxicant. And the brain responds accordingly. It doesn't know how to operate without it. So it sends a firestorm, wave after wave of thoughts and feelings that fluctuate by the minute. Anger. Even blind rage. Well-being followed by intense remorse. Calm, followed by fright. Resolution followed by fear.

Over and over this cycle spun in my head. Especially at night, when the brain forces the body awake to lie there at 3 a.m. with chronic insomnia. This pattern of unrest is why the person is in the most danger in the first few months, especially that initial thirty days. The brain is in a blitzkrieg. Between the artillery coming down and the cravings, the want to go back to the bottle is the greatest. But it won't last forever. That's what the newly sober has to grasp—that this recent horror is only a small part of the process whose symptoms *will begin to fade,* a little less each day after the one month mark. You're still walking up the giant stairwell to escape Hades. But the blue sky is up there, waiting for you as you circle and ascend to the surface.

The weekends were the most dangerous for me at the beginning of the recovery process. The brain remembers this was when you drank the most. And without the work shift, you have plenty of time to sit around and think about it. I played the same mental game that I did during the week. Making it to noon was my first goal on Saturday. Then 3 p.m. Then 6 p.m. 9 p.m. Then a few hours later, I checked off another day on my piece of paper I had hanging on my refrigerator. And I started over again on Sunday.

The first month the cravings were almost constant on the weekends. So I looked at them for what they were. It was a craving, the want of something—nothing more. I ignored them and continued hour by hour. I wasn't in any way ready to go to a gym to lift weights or practice martial arts. So I took long, leisurely walks. Three or four a day sometimes. It was really all I could do. I couldn't sit still to watch a movie, and writing was out of the question as I couldn't concentrate on anything more than a few minutes. But I did read books on alcoholism at short intervals. They were all twelve-step based, telling me theirs was the only protocol that would succeed when I was doing the exact opposite.

One item I noted that first month was that the twelve steppers insisted that *relapse was part of recovery.* I was stunned at this illogic. What did they mean that relapse was part of recovery? Are you kidding me? What in the living hell is that kind of advice to give someone in the first month when the cravings are the worst they will ever be? When the state of mind is in the pits? That's another reason I can't recommend AA, even in the first month. Not with this type of dogma coming from their rooms. Those first few weeks after acute withdrawal, the person is thinking pretty much about nothing except popping open a bottle. They are worn down with insomnia. They are not in a state of mind that has any fortitude. They are in the phase where the highest chance of relapse can occur. And these nitwits take that mindset, as the sponsor shakes his head knowingly, and tells him AA is the only way and that part of the process is *relapse*? Christ, why not just hand the addict the open bottle?

That dogma is the most inept advice I think their entire program contains. So the alcoholic has to hit rock bottom first? Maybe lose his career, his wife and get four DUIs before he is ready to recover? Maybe run a child over and end up in prison? Then he's ready? I mean, I'm sorry to be rude, but are the pundits in AA *completely out of their minds*? That philosophy is asinine. Yes, AA, I get what you are saying. You're not saying to relapse. You're saying the relapse has to hit rock bottom eventually, and then you can come back. Well, that just gives ammunition to the person's psyche to go ahead and get there before getting better. It says, sure, I still have my job and wife—everything isn't wholly lost yet. Maybe I'm not ready yet to stop drinking. Let me keep hitting that bottle until I've relapsed a few more times and destroyed everything that mattered to me. Oh, I'm finally home-less and wanted by the police—now I can start.

I have a better idea. How about defeating the addiction the second you realize you have a problem? How about instead of calling yourself diseased for the rest of your life, you attempt to examine why you started drinking in the first place? Like the Prentiss foundation does—with an eighty percent cure rate, mind you, long term. How about putting it initially in your head that you are *never* going to touch the offending substance again. That you are going to recreate your life from one of an addict to one who is cured and sober? That's the mindset I want you to begin to build while you make your way to the thirty day mark.

Who the hell came up with "relapse is part of recovery" and made it the ulti-mate truth? Relapse is relapse. Once you quit alcohol, that should be it. You never go back. Because if you do relapse, you might not get a second chance. But that's what the sages with their majority of failures keep propagating and they do it in that first month. They are planting in the brain of the vulnerable, newly sober that they probably will fall backward as *relapse is part of recovery*. So the newly sober never place into their thought patterns that they will never touch alcohol again. They develop a neural pattern that *maybe* they will never touch it. Or maybe they will. They will sit in a circle, sucking those cigarettes, hiding from life and state that they are sober today—but they don't know about tomorrow.

Nonsense. I knew about tomorrow, even in the first month of sobriety. Just like I knew when I quit on January 22nd, 2009, that January 23rd, 2009, I would not touch alcohol again. And I knew about next year. And today, I know about twenty years from now. I made a conscious decision that I wouldn't again tip the bottle to my lips. I knew I was still in the inferno the first thirty days into my cure. And I knew it would eventually pass. You can't drink heavily in an alcoholic man-ner for the last thirteen years and expect to walk out without a scratch. That loan shark has to be paid with long building interest. But telling myself it was a maybe? That I didn't know what the next month held? Rubbish. I told myself that I was disowning my Dutch Uncle Buddy. I was through with him forever.

No, AA, relapse is *not* part of recovery. Maybe you think that because so many, under your guidelines, do relapse. But so few actually recover, do they? Again, the majority fail. And a huge number fail in that first month. As you sit, smoking in your rooms, chanting the mantra that doesn't work. They don't re-cover. That's because your mantra of "relapse is a part of recovery" is an oxymo-ron. They didn't need to fail over and over before coming to your rooms. If they had followed my advice, they would have succeeded the first time without ever stepping through your doors.

It doesn't matter whether you go to a rehab center for the first month or AA or continue to go to work every day as I did. You can stick yourself in a cabin in the wilderness, far from society, if you want. You are still going to go through the misery of the emotional ride and intense nonstop cravings that first month and sometimes two. It comes down to that willpower again. No matter what avenue you take, you will want to reach for the bottle. But you choose not to. That is the only way to recover. You don't touch it again. And after significant time passes, that choice will be as natural as the drinking once was. If you hold to your guns, you will one day be able to say: *I was once an alcoholic. Today, I am not. I am cured.*

The above declaration is the exact opposite doctrine that they program you with the first week in AA, where the permanent members circle like hawks with their evangelistic code of *This is the only way.* The newly sober person already feels god awful from the depression that is descending in that first month. His ego is shattered as he realizes what he has done to himself. Then the first thing he hears is he will always be an addict. He will always be diseased. That there is no end to recovery. Recovery is ongoing and forever. He will never be free from it. It is his new master status—he is an *addict.* For the rest of his days. Never mind that thing called self-worth. Do you think you're going to live as an independent being by using AA? A strong soul who has beaten the addiction? *Nope—you're an addict, do you hear—always an addict. If you leave us, you'll fall back. You can never recover. Oh, and by the way—relapse can be a part of recovery.*

And this is what AA will do in the first thirty days. When the person is out of the acute stage, the brain is well enough to analyze the addiction but emotionally sick enough to be brainwashed with the twelve-step mantra. The almighty steps, burned forever in stone. And one of two things happen. One, the person returns to drinking as most in AA do. Two, the person remains in the minority and does not drink but traps himself forever in AA. Or you go to your grave early as Knapp did. Does Knapp sound like a win, AA? To me, she resembles a tragedy.

I went through it alone as I find nothing useful about AA. After two weeks,

I had read a few books on twelve-step recovery. And I didn't buy any of it. I rode the roller coaster that initial period after the acute phase. It was a rough ride too. It would rise slowly then drop you into a descent of depression. Turn you upside down with panic attacks and anxiety. Spin you every which way with severe agitation, which seemed unrelenting. Then suddenly, I would feel good for an hour. Then it would start all over. Compounded by sleep deprivation, thanks to chronic insomnia. Somehow, I didn't think sitting in a circle, telling my story and listening to everyone else's descent was going to make me feel any better.

After a few weeks, I looked upon the internet to see if there were any chat type rooms with AA. I found they do have AA meetings online. Why not? I had to occupy myself every night anyway and couldn't sit long enough to get through an episode of *The Sopranos*. No one even had to know my name. So I made a screen handle to log on and dropped in one night. And there they were, from all over the world. On top of their physical meetings in the rooms and calls to sponsors, they went home and then did AA on the net. I watched the chat comments for a while and then typed in that I was two weeks sober and had never gone to a meeting nor intended to. I did have some questions about how long could I expect the roller coaster ride to last? The cult flooded the laptop screen. Unanimous decision resounded that I would never make it. I was doomed. The AA way was the only way.

I clicked off.

So I continued on day after day. Hyper anxiety persisted most nights. Only small segments of well-being existed in-between the severe, black depression. I took the perspective of it for what it was. It was lack of natural flowing opiates that were used to being released via alcohol. It would take time for them to regulate themselves as nature intended. The rest was a cranial illusion. These were just feelings. One can ignore feelings as one can the cravings. I was in a storm, but I had set the vessel in the right direction. I would reach the shoreline one day. But I had to pass through the tempest first. The triggers for alcohol remained all around me the second I left the apartment. Even grocery shopping, as I passed the aisle lined with shelf after shelf of the cold, golden wheat in the glass and can.

I ignored those bottles and cans—they were no longer part of my life. Willpower. The people in AA could be forever addicts. I wouldn't be. I kept getting through the weekends, segment by segment. One Sunday, I even went bowling to pass the time. And people were drinking even there. I realized that avoidance wasn't the answer. That's what the people in the rooms did. They hid from the world of social triggers. I would learn to live with them. And today, ninety-five percent of the time I am unaffected when I see a bottle of beer popped and poured in the lounge as I sip my soda water with two limes. The other five percent of periodic cravings, I continue to ignore. I've done it so many times it is now an ingrained habit.

Because today I'm cured of the addiction. I'm cured because I built these neural pathways in that first month.

I think the first-weekend after the acute withdrawal was the most challenging. Once I made it through that Saturday and Sunday, I knew I could do it again. When the two-week mark had passed, I was on new ground. Even in my competitive bodybuilding days, in my early twenties, I had never gone two full weeks without alcohol, even if it was just a few beers.

After the first two weeks had passed, the nurse who had witnessed what appeared to be a dying man at day four noted that my color was much better. Even with the mental upheaval and insomnia, I had been eating a decent diet, filled with fruits and vegetables. I looked into the mirror. I *did* look better after just a few weeks. Even with the sleep deprivation, the lines in my face seemed slightly faded. Emotionally, I was still a train wreck. But I didn't have that haggard countenance any more.

The third week came and passed. Suddenly, I was nearing the revered thirty-day mark. Where if I were in rehab, they would be planning my discharge back to the world. Where if in AA, they would give me the first chip. I began to notice something else as well. The cravings were letting up. Not a lot, but there were a few hours in the day now where I didn't have them at all. I didn't have a running need every single minute of the day to suck the golden liquid down. Instead of the spells being the constant, mouth-watering freight trucks that circled the block, the cravings became more episodic. The intensity of them remained but was beginning to lessen just slightly as well. There were one or two hours in the day when I, for the first time in over a decade, knew what it was like to feel normal. *This is what regular people felt like,* I had thought. No driving urge to pop that cap on the bottle every day. *So even in just a few weeks, I was already feeling better.*

I wasn't off the roller coaster yet. I don't think I slept more than five hours a night, at most, that first month. My skin always seemed to be twitchy and itched a lot. I still couldn't sit still to read a book or write. But day thirty finally arrived. And it felt no different than day twenty-nine.

I called two of my friends and let them know that I had finally quit it. That I was in Hell, but I had stopped. They were stunned that I had done this alone. I hadn't told anyone except the AA chat room at two weeks in of my cessation. What could my friends say except to hang in there? They had watched me drink myself away for years.

I revisited that AA online room at day thirty. The same screen names were there. The same subjects of today's meeting were yesterday's meeting—and what steps they were on. The same mantras from the same sages who had been sober for ten years and never let go of the hand that reached from AA. I asked if anyone remembered me? They did. I told them I had now reached day thirty. And that I still hadn't gone to a meeting. The hyper responses lit the screen once again. They told me I would never make it alone.

Click.

I had now read three or four books on twelve steppers and AA. I also had been to their online support. These people weren't helpful. They were cult-like. They weren't happy I had made thirty days. They were angry I had done it without them. My cutting loose from the chains of alcoholism only reminded them that they were still trapped. They wanted me to fail. So they could say; *see, relapse is part of recovery. Now let's work on that first step. You're an addict. You will always be an addict.* They weren't happy for me at all. They were enraged.

The AA people in the books and sites in that first thirty days began to remind me a lot of the faith-healing evangelists I had known in rural Indiana, who passed through from time to time. For these people, it didn't matter if you believed in God, it had to be through their rituals, their guidelines. You had to throw up your hands in their presence, or you weren't a Christian, according to them. The proponents of AA are very similar. They do not want you to be a whole person. They want you, in your mind, to believe you are forever an addict—that you cannot survive without them. Even when you point out that most of their own don't survive in the program at all.

Almost everyone who attempts recovery goes to AA. And I can understand Bill Wilson and Dr. Bob Smith's need for a safe haven when AA started. In past times, men were expected to drink. You weren't considered a man unless you did, as Jack London noted in his autobiography, *John Barleycorn*, his most significant barrier to cease drinking was the constant peer pressure from other men in his youth. By the time he made it as a writer and could seclude himself, it was too late. So Wilson and Smith set up the safe house where men could go day or night to escape.

But today, no one really cares whether you drink or not, even if you are a rugged man. If you have a Coke at a party when everyone else is drinking beer, you might get a raised eyebrow or two of suspicion. *Is he an alcoholic?* They might whisper this inquiry among themselves. People don't know what to say. They are afraid they may offend you by asking. So they casually ask why you don't drink when they already suspect why. I always handled it easily. I never denied being an alcoholic when I was one. I don't deny sobriety either. I tell them I used to be an alcoholic—and now I'm not. Then I tell them I don't go to AA, by the way. That my cure is I don't drink anymore. If they ask if it was hard, I tell them the body and spirit went through Hell and now it's done.

So I had hit thirty days, and the mental anguish was the same. Unlike the five days of acute withdrawal, the next estimate of evolution wasn't an exact science. Day forty-five was the turning point for me. I noted day forty-five very well in my journal. It was the first day that I actually felt *good*. Not just for an hour either, for the entire day as if a continent had rolled off my shoulders. I had no anxiety and no agitation that day. And for the first time, there were no incessant cravings for the juice. Even when I passed the neon signs and billboards. How strange it was to have this sensation when only a month and a half ago I would be waking up every morning to the usual sickness. The vertigo when I stepped on an elevator in the hospital the first few hours of the morning. Now the only physical symptoms I had were occasional stabbings of pain in my liver and kidneys, which were becoming less frequent as the recovery continued.

More importantly, crossing the thirty-day mark into the second month was a huge mental leap. If I made it past a month, I could do it five more times to get to the next landmark. Six months. And if the former addict passes that milestone, they say he has a good chance to stay sober.

In the initial phase, I had resolutely decided not to touch alcohol again. But I couldn't picture a life without it. I couldn't imagine that today, well over a decade later, I would write about the experience, which was now long ago. At day forty-five, however, I *could* begin to imagine the alcohol free existence. My thirty days took a month and a half for this to happen in my mind.

Many in the traditional twelve steps never even make it this far. The rehab center releases them at day thirty, and the cravings persist as the staff tells them they will always be addicts. The confirmation given that they will always be sick. Then instructed that relapse may be part of recovery. They are surrounded for a month by those who clearly state that you never know if you will be sober tomorrow and only today matters. Well, tomorrow *does* matter. And many tomorrows from now as well. I wasn't going to keep referring to myself as an *addict*. The addict can't stop. I had stopped for forty-five days. And I wasn't going back. I was sober today. And I knew I would be when the sun rose again.

I was a physical therapist who believed in holistic recovery. A global bringing back of the person who existed long before the substance abuse began. And I couldn't recover by regurgitating tragedy in AA every night while sucking on the cigarettes that killed Carolyn Knapp. I didn't bother going online this time to the AA chat room to let the pundits know I had made it well past the thirty-day mark and was now at forty-five and finally felt fine for a whole day. I didn't have a chip in my pocket, noting the time that had passed. I didn't give any speech in front of fellow addicts who gripped their coffee cups. And I knew that I wouldn't feel fine every day in the long protracted withdrawal.

The protracted withdrawal lasts for up to two years while the system rebalances itself. But the initial onslaught of neurological chaos was over. I knew there would still be days when I would feel rotten. And they would become less and less in frequency over time. I had walked out of the inferno and poked my head above the surface in the cool air. I didn't recognize the world I had left behind not too long ago. And I had disregarded the traditional safe house they offered to hide from this unfamiliar terrain. Could an ex-alcoholic of only forty-five days live in an alcohol-filled world, unaided by AA and the twelve steps? They told me it was impossible. And I hadn't been sober long enough to prove them wrong.

I was exhausted. The chronic insomnia had taken its toll. I was tired, but the mind was clear. I tactically began to plan the next phase. The rejuvenation of body and spirit that would take me to the next level, which would eventually lead to complete recovery and cure.

Compensation strategies are used to combat the internal remnants of childhood trauma. I had used the arena of physical prowess as mine. And the numbing effects of alcohol to pretend all was well when nothing was. One doesn't have to deal with dysfunction if he can drown it every night in booze. It cures mental pain that is not addressed by position, title, money or being a formidable fighter. Over time, alcohol eliminates the daily physical pain as well, as with enough years of abuse, the body is now corporeally addicted to the poison.

I felt terrific that day of forty-five. And then the high came down, and a steady black depression descended. The demons had risen to the surface and showed what had led to the thirteen years of heavy abuse. And even before that, back to June of 1986 when I used the analgesic in large amounts for the first time to mask pain. The first time the anxiety of past trauma was artificially removed. A time when at any given night that I wanted it gone, the anesthesia was usually only a few blocks away.

So I decided I had a choice for the next phase of recovery—the recovery that would eventually cure me of the addiction forever. I could run to AA and admit my error to their condescending, nodding heads, where they would tell me I would never recover. Where they would inform that I would always be an addict. And that I could expect possible relapse. Or I could completely rebuild the Self. I could create a new person. A sober person. A non-addict. Someone who was cured. The shakes, rattles and rolls of the initial month and a half had worn off. Now the depression encompassed me. Depression can lead the newly sober right back to the bottle. And why was there depression? Because the natural opiates of life weren't dropping from the brain.

I had broken the thirty-day mark and more days were steadily being ticked off. My next phase of recovery would be to the six-month line in the sand.

Now that I was somewhat out of the edges of the typhoon, I could begin the road back. I could start to search for a path of normality. I wasn't going to go to a psychotherapist who would hand me a prescription for antidepressants, which never relieve the person of his affliction. I would holistically begin to recreate the body and spirit.

SYNOPSIS: PHASE TWO TO THIRTY DAYS
One will walk through a physiological hell during the acute withdrawal stage. It lasts for about five days almost on cue. You could mark the second stage as finished at day thirty. In reality, it will last somewhere from the thirty to sixty-day milestone. You'll know the end of that phase when you have the first day you can say you feel good. For as much as the acute withdrawal is a torment of the physical, the post-acute is a trial of the mental.

The emotions are on a wild roller coaster. Thoughts of suicide are common with a side dish of deep depression. An hour of euphoria is matched by six of anxiety. Night terrors come and go as panic attacks ride over you during the day. The key to getting through this is understanding it is just your neurochemical system going haywire. These emotions will calm down over time. You must comprehend that this is another level in Dante's oven. You may still feel horrible this month. A few more from now, you won't.

The cravings will be at their worst for the next thirty days or so. Even when they are no longer constant, down the road they will come and go for months and even a year or two until they finally become infrequent and minuscule. They will never be like the first month, though. Almost every thought in the second phase will be on alcohol. And everything around you will ignite that thought. It would be an excellent idea to stay away from everything related to alcohol in the second stage. I warrant this advice for many months for some newly recovering. For me, I was out at day eleven in a lounge with alcohol right at the table. I also have tremendous willpower. And I needed every ounce of it that night. I should have stayed home.

Self-isolation isn't the worst idea in the first month. If AA had a weaning off program instead of permanence to AA protocol, I would advise initially going to their meetings. But I can't advise a mantra that is unhealthy with a track record that places the recovering addict right back into harm's way. There is a time when you are a recovering addict. And then there is a time when you can claim cure. You are in the recovering phase in the first thirty days. As well as up to the two year mark. The rest is simply following the contract you made with yourself when you finally threw the alcohol into the refuse box for good.

You're going to have a lot of insomnia in the second phase. Then suddenly, you'll have a few days of hypersomnia. Then back and forth between the two. For me, the first month and a half, I had much more insomnia than hypersomnia. These types of sleep dysfunctions will pass—as well as the nightmares that you will have.

If you have any energy to exercise, that is wonderful. I didn't. That came in the third phase of my recovery. I did take half-hour walks, though, which technically is light exercise. Sometimes more than once a day. The walks were just something to get the constant jitters out of the system, which is always good. But that was about all I did for exercise for that first month and a half.

My contradiction will be, on the one hand, I say don't eat a lot of sugar or use caffeine. In the ideal situation, it would be great to start right on a healthy diet immediately after the acute stage. But you are in the phase where the cravings are the worst and most constant that they are ever going to be until the addict is considered cured. My advice here is to do the best you can. You put a lot of vegetables and fruits in your system and a lot of water. And whole grains and decent protein. Don't eat a lot of fast food. You need nutrients that make you feel better, not worse. I drank no soft drinks or caffeinated power drinks or the like. I did have about four to five cups of coffee a day. And after work, I always had one or two of those milkshakes. I probably smoked five to seven cigarettes a day. I phased them all out later. I state that sugar, nicotine and caffeine will induce cravings. But the fact is, you aren't going to get out of having mouth-watering want for alcohol no matter what you do in phase two.

So on the other hand, I used what I needed until that magic day arrived—forty-five. Then I phased the unhealthy things out. I limit sugar and coffee today as it affects mood swings and can accelerate depression. Most of the time, I am not depressed. I want to keep it that way. And unlike Carolyn Knapp, smoking was not a major part of my cure. It isn't even a minor part today as I do not smoke at all. And was Knapp ever cured? No, remember—she was in continuous recovery. And she died young—still in it.

You do whatever you have to do to get through the second phase. If going to a putt-putt course every night gets you through it, then it does. Or maybe it's trying to watch the entire series of *Family Guy* and hitting that milkshake at night. Laughter does seem to make things better.

This stage of the recovery process is not the time to reflect on why you ended up in this condition or to beat yourself to a pulp for getting there. You can evaluate this when your system calms down. The only thing you have to focus on now and forever is following your contract. That's it. The acute phase and the post-acute thirty-day phase are the most internally chaotic. You only have to ride those first steps out once—and not drink.

At the end of this phase, whether it is on point at day thirty or forty-five, like for myself, will be when the physical and mental reformation can begin to be analyzed. By now, the addict has gone through the acute physical withdrawal and the tsunami of psychological withdrawal. Now, the former addict is ready to advance toward the cure.

CHAPTER 5

REACHING THE SURFACE

The estimated thirty-day mark, when the heaviest emotional symptoms of post-acute withdrawal begin to abate, varies with the person. The physical torment of the acute phase itself can almost be guaranteed to last to the exact hour of the completion of five days. The next phase will fluctuate among the recently sober. For me, the door opened on day forty-five. Day forty-five was grand. Many days afterward wouldn't be. But every day that passed was now another brick that stacked for the foundation of a new life.

If AA wasn't so dogmatic in their mantra and protocols, maybe their rooms would be an okay place to reside for six months after the last drop. The only two AA meetings I ever attended were close to one year sober. I had brought someone to those gatherings to show her that there was a problem with her own addiction. I knew they would all circle in their continuous "storytelling," but I wanted her to hear the tales so she would recognize their biographies and hers were the same. I also wanted to see their philosophy in action. After the meeting, I told her to never go back to the rooms. She took my advice. She is years sober today.

Is it true that dark spirits rise from childhood during the first six months of sobriety? Yes. They do, and they have razor-sharp teeth. Almost all former alcoholics had trauma in childhood, which makes me doubt the genetic factor as the primary role player. And maybe there are genetic predispositions. But then AA calls alcoholism a disease. Alcoholism isn't a disease. It is an addiction. Cancer is a disease. Drinking alcohol is a choice. Your body is very sick when you are an alcoholic. But the alcoholic is only mentally diseased at the time *because* of his addiction. And unlike cancer, you alone can cure it.

The AA meetings could have a purpose in the initial hundred and eighty days. Maybe it would be a good idea to tell your story so you understand why the addiction happened. Maybe, even in the beginning, you need the nicotine to get you through. Even I used cigarettes periodically at times in the early phases of recovery.

But then these terrible physical and emotional habits never stop with the minority who stay sober in the AA guidebook. Their lives are a collage of cigarettes, coffee and rehashing the past in-between the *Serenity Prayer* and next stop point step under the guidance of the sponsor. And by the way, AA, what happens after the twelve steps are completed? Ah, you may fall backward. Because relapse is part of recovery, right? Because according to your mantra, the recovery is never complete, and you are always an addict. What a dismal philosophy to live by for the rest of your life.

I contend the premise of AA is nonsense. Again, I don't have to prove my point. AA's recidivism rates prove it for me. I beat alcoholism. I have well passed that decade mark of being sober. I have had not one single drink in all of that time—not one. And I didn't do it by living in the past of alcoholism but by reconstructing my life and outlook for the future. A spiritual revolution that began as soon as the initial withdrawal period ended. The third phase is where you can really start the total reinvention of your brand new self.

Cravings were still there to that six-month mark but now more at intervals instead of the constant salivating for the hops that you will experience in the second phase. And I had beaten them enough in the last month and a half that ignoring them was now a new habit. I didn't tell my mind that relapse was part of recovery. I told my mind I would disregard the cravings forever. So when they hit, I simply waited for them to pass. There was no reason to cave in to them. I had ignored them in a much worse state during the first month sober. A time when the cravings were almost constant. Ignoring them with intervals in-between was much easier. Mornings and early afternoons were now craving free. And when they would hit in the evenings and nights, they would last for an hour to an hour and a half. Then they dissipated. The craving is the greatest threat to cure. But they were decreasing in frequency and intensity. There was no reason to think they wouldn't continue to do so with time. So that's what I focused on: *It would continue to get easier with time.*

Hypersomnia replaced insomnia with greater frequency at times. Suddenly, I went from sleeping four or five hours a night to eleven. This influx helped to get through the idle weekends for sure. On Saturdays and Sundays, I slept until 11 a.m. Followed by naps in the late afternoon. Then all night again. Then insomnia would return for a week. Then it would vanish. And return for a week a month later.

I no longer had horrific nightmares every night. But the dreams were strange and vivid. Many of them were about childhood. I dreamed of family members I hadn't spoken to for over twenty years and people I had completely disconnected from shortly after high school. I had disowned that abusive family when I was twenty. I knew at seventeen, I would walk away from these toxic people the day my grandfather, an honorable man, would be taken by the emphysema that had plagued him for the last ten years. He finally died when I was in basic training for the Army Reserve. And that was the last time I spoke to any of them. They got my letter in Virginia stating I was through with their bloodline forever. But a lot of those memories rose up as I made my way to six months and beyond.

The agitation wasn't so severe in the third phase. The anxiety operated much like the cravings did in the next few months—more episodic than constant. There were periods of calm and then periods of anger. Even rage. Sometimes a homicidal tide at nothing in particular would flow inland. And then it would recede. I realized it was an illusion. The brain was trying to relearn how to function without the intoxicant. And it would throw forward every emotion while it figured it out. But when these mental sensations did arise, I knew they would be followed by on and off normality. Intermittent periods of peace, which was a far better deal than the constant emotional inferno I had just escaped. I wondered what it would be like a year from now? Would the roller coaster eventually level itself, with only occasional bumps and slow, smooth turns? The only way to find out was to let it ride.

I had already started a semi healthy diet once the acute five-day withdrawal ended. Two large salads, several pieces of fruit and decent protein supplemented meats, matched by whole grains were now my regular daily food stocks. After the second phase, I began to focus a great deal more on negation of toxins along with my proper diet. I got the coffee down to just a few cups a day. I slowly eliminated cigarettes. I kept the ice cream but limited it to once a day now. And I downsized the fast food to once a week at most. Also, I drank water. Lots of water versus Cokes and other soft drink beverages. To this day, I rarely touch a soda.

I also don't ever consume "energy drinks." Red Bull is certainly not needed to get through the sun's sweep through the daylight hours. If the body was to continue to repair itself, it required the essential natural vitamins and minerals. The diet is the cement to the concrete foundation on which to build one's new house.

Then I returned to exercise and built my routine back up to five days a week. My involvement in fitness had been sporadic over the last six years since I ceased my attempts to go pro in Thai boxing at thirty-four. It doesn't matter what type of exercise one engages in as long as its nature is cardiovascular oriented. For me, it was my old, Thai boxing routine of ten to thirteen rounds. I also added weight lifting on top of the program. I spend an hour and fifteen minutes to an hour and a half in the gym per session. One doesn't have to lift weights as I do. But the cardio program is essential, whether it is a treadmill, boxing or Zumba.

When I started the third phase of recovery, I was still very fatigued, even after forty-five days sober. At two months into sobriety, I began to go to the gym three times a week for a month. Then I built that frequency up to four and later increased back to my former regular routine of five times a week. The first week of exercise, I was very sore. The next few weeks, I continued to feel extremely fatigued. Then energy began to build. I was taking steps to walk back to a lifestyle of health and fitness.

This exercise program accomplishes a few things. First, it is just physically healthy for the person. Everyone, whether a former alcoholic or not, should engage in some program like this as we have a severe sedentary problem in the United States today. Anxiety levels in this nation have skyrocketed with a variety of stress and obesity-related diagnoses, which are really nothing more than most Americans sitting on the couch after work and on the weekends. For the former alcoholic, the cardio exercise program will recalibrate the blood pressure to normal levels. Smoking cigarettes at AA every night will not.

The vigorous physical exercise will also help alleviate the black depression every newly sober person feels due to lack of proper opiate dumpage. And during that first two years, the depression will be like a bad mother-in-law who visits entirely too often and stays for extended periods. But if you are at the gym, you are filling your evening hours, which keeps you from thinking about drinking. The endorphins that will drop during exercise will decrease the cravings as well as the other mental symptoms of protracted withdrawal. The reason why is because exercise generally makes you feel good. No matter what the circumstances, life doesn't nearly look as hopeless when one is soaked with sweat after finishing a super accelerated Pilates session. And that calm you achieve with exercise will usually stay with you throughout the evening and night.

Exercise seems to accelerate the want to throw the pack of cigarettes away like you did the beer can. When you start living in a holistically healthy manner, it suddenly becomes easy to continue choices that walk right in line with that healthy lifestyle. So if you had to smoke cigarettes in the prior phase to get through it, this is the time to quit them. The exercise program, matched by the clean diet and elimination of harmful substances, is the core of recovery. Or you can sit in the rooms, smoking one death stick after another, pouring coffee down while you talk about how bad your life was in the days of alcoholism. Has anyone ever left an AA meeting feeling grand? In the two times I went, I sure as hell didn't.

During the third phase, I also added other highly physical activities to my life for the days I wasn't at the gym. I engaged in day hikes into the wilderness and even weekend trips. Once, I took a rock climbing class. I went fishing in the lakes of the northwest. Snowshoeing and skiing in the winter. I signed up for a Tough Mudder fitness event in Maine one summer while contracting. You can afford all of these things. Most outdoor activities require a small park fee if anything at all. You used to spend thousands a year on your habit for Christ's sake. The cravings will still be there in phase three and well past it. But if you keep yourself busy with endorphin dropping physical activities all of the time, they will be far less than walking through an emotional twelve steps. Not to mention, you will be a far healthier person as well. Maybe you'll become a triathlete. Or climb Mount Everest. I can promise you won't be holistically healthy if you keep regurgitating your pitiful story six nights a week in the meeting house.

I also added a meditative component to my recovery program. I used this weapon to fight the anxiety, which would sometimes rise to the level of full-scale panic attacks. This technique would be a calming of the mind, controlled breathing type of regiment. I had done a little yoga in the past. Also, Zen meditation. Today, I rely on Tai Chi, yoga and meditative breathing. All three put together take about twenty minutes after I come home from the gym. Some people use prayer meditation. That method may work with some as long as the former addict doesn't believe he is powerless over his past addiction. After thirty days, you have proven you do have the power not to pick up the bottle. All you have to do now is continue to walk toward the cure. But you have to have something in your tool-box, meditatively speaking. There has to be something in your arsenal to quiet the mind. And a meditative program will do that.

There have been times when I have used the above to reverse an oncoming anxiety attack completely. Or at least turned the intensity of it down. It can be used to battle insomnia as well. A calm state of mind decreases the cravings in that first six months. You may still have them, but the frequency will be less, I guarantee. And like the exercise program above, the meditative additive to recovery also aids in reducing depression. You don't even need to join a Tai Chi or yoga studio. The internet and bookstore can be a resource for these recovery aids.

After the roller coaster levels off, the depression remains—long after the last drops of alcohol evaporated over a month to a month and a half prior. Suddenly, the mind is now reconnected to the soul. The walled, numbing agent that kept the two separate has been knocked down by the torrential winds from the hurricane, which has now dissipated. And what is left is wreckage. But the former addict can now think clearly in the new periodic bouts of extended calm.

At forty-five days, this was the first time I felt good since ending Mr. Barleycorn's life. I also felt I was now turning the corner into the next phase of recovery. I thought about day one. Day one, I was officially an ex-alcoholic on paper. But that day, just a month and a half prior, I would have never been able to comprehend getting through this allotment of time without alcohol. In this phase, I could now foresee getting through the rest of my life without it. But now the mind has to contemplate why the addiction ever took hold, to begin with. A great deal of solving the coming depression will be to finally acknowledge the past—and putting it in the grave with the barley forever. This process only begins in the third phase. It will take time.

AA believes in living in the past. The past trauma never ends for them. They are still living in the wreck of their former lives. They tell their story over and over about how they came to be an alcoholic and then chant the mantra. They believe themselves to be diseased still—ten years well after the last drink. They remain to hold the status of sick in their minds. They believe it was a genetic time bomb that was bound to go off.

I don't believe the origin of their addiction was genetic. I contend most of them had trauma of some sort in their childhoods—and usually learned the behavior of substance abuse from their parents. They speak of their childhoods a great deal and then walk out of the rooms, stating that yes—they will always be addicts. That addiction lies right outside the doors of AA if they don't remain enclosed in the meetings every night. And as they are telling their stories in the same circle, they never equate that *childhood trauma is what made them the addict. That if they can understand the nature of where the addiction truly originated and come to grips with it once and for all, they will no longer feel the compulsion toward substance abuse.* This is why in this reconstructive phase it is crucially important to understand the depression. Yes, the brain is in flux from the sudden cessation of alcohol. But more importantly, the key to never returning to the addiction is *to understand the real root of it.*

Experts universally agree that children of trauma carry the effects into adulthood. And many counter these aftereffects by becoming alcoholics or drug addicts. Normality was not taught to these children. Social abnormality in relationships is the lesson plan for these types of dysfunctional families. This phenomenon explains why an abused daughter marries a future abuser. There is familiarity in their learned version of "normal," even if it is far from it. The mind pattern has been programmed to walk through a thorn filled side path while everyone else strolls on the open trail. And the ugly, unmarked route leads to the dark forest where the victim wanders alone. They don't know what the source of pain is, only that they are in constant turmoil. They are living in a world where they cannot assimilate. So they attempt to control their existence by compensation strategies. Some become corporate successes. Or long-time martial artists and fighters like myself. It gives the illusion of control over a world where they exist alone.

But the inner turbulence remains with these people. Relationships are chaotic and fail quickly. Or the person is unable even to begin one. Seclusion is common. The survivor doesn't understand why—for all appears normal on the outside world. I had beaten my childhood and was now a medical contractor. By all means, everything looked standard. But internally, I was still a traumatized child, frozen in time. And how does the now-adult handle the inward chaos? Substance abuse is many times the answer for the former traumatized.

For myself, physical prowess became the unconscious compensation strategy. When I was fourteen, I weighed a hundred pounds, had steel-rimmed glasses and a hyperactive personality. As I stated in the first chapter, I was an easy victim for a pack of boys at an elite Jesuit run secondary school. To say they picked on me wouldn't even begin to describe my time there. I was terrorized for three years. This trauma occurred at school and then at home with my father. It lightened up at school as I had discovered bodybuilding at fourteen and was getting bigger by the month. But it was still there until the day I left for Norfolk.

By the time I was twenty, I wasn't a thin, helpless kid any longer. I was a competitive bodybuilder who was beginning to discover martial arts. And I was in the Army Reserve. Ten years later, I could say I had served on a long-range reconnaissance team in Intelligence and was an assistant instructor in Thai boxing. I had fought in thirteen full contact school run events. And a few years after that had even managed to become an independent medical contractor as a physical therapist.

And these were the compensation strategies, mainly these superphysical feats. But they didn't cure the broken child. The alcohol gave the illusion that it did. The alcohol kept me from realizing there was nothing to prove. The alcohol kept me wanting to join the Marines at thirty-four and drop into Afghanistan. Luckily, the Marines operated in reality and declined to accept aging vets. My diseased mind did not share that same rationale.

The Self would have to be reconstructed and the long-frozen child thawed out so his legs could begin to run and finally catch up to adulthood. If the transition could take place, I could bury the past trauma for good. And if put it into the ground, then the need to pour the anesthesia over its gravestone would be eliminated. For the demon would finally be dead forever.

All of these realizations came with the beginning of the third phase of recovery. Now that the mind could somewhat think clearly, I could start to focus on the long path that led me to the final precipice of alcoholism in the late stages. It is very common for prior addicts to continue to have massive depression and anxiety for years, maybe for the rest of their lives, once they quit drinking. I firmly believe that the AA protocol is laying the foundation for these continued catastrophic mindsets. If you start the process of repairing the neural pathways from the childhood past in the third phase, when the brain finally recalibrates at the end of the two year protracted withdrawal, much of the expected depressive and anxiety episodes will end.

Will the former addict, as I claim myself to be, still feel cravings after he finally thrusts the sword into his childhood demon? Sure. He will still have them a great deal in the third phase up to six months. And he will have them throughout the long protracted phase to two years. He will have them even after he claims cure. It is easier for the addict if he understands why these cravings are occurring. And that answer isn't because he was born with a disease called alcoholism.

The body became physically addicted to the offending substance as well as emotionally addicted. Alcohol was used to solve pain in most cases. Only after years of abuse, did the physical component come into play. The cured will still have deep memory triggers that are activated with certain stimuli. They become less with time—in frequency and intensity. Stressful situations in life reactivate them in full force for me to this day. And they recede. The key is to understand that probably for the rest of the former addict's life, he will have to deal with cravings periodically. And the answer continues to be the same—ignore them. Because you made a pact with yourself that you will never touch alcohol again.

You will note the cravings start to decrease after the initial month or month and a half. And that reduction only continues with time. And here is a wake-up call. AA can't make them disappear completely either. As a matter of fact, it was after my two brief encounters with AA that I had two intense cravings. I was eleven months into sobriety at the time. Who wouldn't want a drink after being in that negative environment where all they talk about is alcohol?

So my routine would be to go to the gym five days a week and afterwards to engage in the meditative and spiritual work for about twenty minutes. And ingest a healthy diet of essential minerals and vitamins all day long. Insomnia and hypersomnia cycles began to decrease as I returned to normal sleep rhythms, just like everyone else.

I hiked trails on the weekends in addition to my regular fitness program. The wilderness has its own healing effect. Again, I highly recommend outdoor activities as much as possible. The fresh air and sun alone do wonders. If you live near any national parks, then frequent them as much as you can. Or drive a hundred miles to get there. Turn your life into one of activity—of *living*, trying to absorb everything nature has to offer. That alone will have a unique effect on recovery.

During the last few months before the hundred and eighty-day mark, I got to do something most people don't. I departed on a series of backpacking adventures into the wilderness mountains. One expedition landed me on the infamous John Muir Trail. On July 22nd, 2009, after crossing eight high altitude peaks on a two hundred and twenty-mile path, I stood on top of Mount Whitney at over fourteen thousand feet of elevation. It was the six-month mark of my recovery. I wasn't telling my story and getting a chip in a crowded room. I was breathing the cold air through my nostrils, standing on iron legs on one of the toughest trails in America.

Even at the six month mark, I didn't exist in the alcoholic past. I was living today. I looked down at the valleys, dropping from the ridgelines in the distance. I had made six months. And that was the moment when I was certain that I was going to be alcohol-free the rest of my life. Maybe you can't take months off for something like this epic ending at the six-month milepost. Take a week or two then. Or a long weekend. Something that aggressively signifies that you have risen from the dead. A flag raised which waves vigorously that you have conquered new terrain and are winning the war. A testament under the stars that you are a spirit reborn.

Or you can go to a meeting, tell your story of your miserable past and get another chip to put in your pocket while smoking that cigarette.

My novel habits were becoming ingrained. My new custom was *not* to feel ill in the morning. My new routine was to go to the gym most nights instead of the liquor store. I looked at the self-taken snapshots of myself all along the John Muir Trail. I compared those pictures to my older alcoholic passport image. I didn't look like the same person. My new photos showed someone who appeared a decade younger, rather than the harrowed, red flushed countenance that the old picture portrayed from the passport photo office, long before my last shared drop with Uncle Buddy. The person I saw on the Muir looked relaxed. Vibrant. Alive. As far as the demon? He was starting to suffocate under the weight of my recovery program.

All of my research said the protracted withdrawal would last, at most, twenty-four months. I stood on top of Whitney with six now laid to rest. Even AA, the program they stated I would never make it without, said you had a good chance at six months. The next part of the journey was the long voyage to the two-year mark. It was still rough seas, but it looked as if I was finally out of the storm.

SYNOPSIS: THIRD PHASE TO SIX MONTHS

I state that this phase begins at the thirty-day mark of sobriety, but in reality, it could be somewhere between thirty to sixty days. As I have said, my thirty-day mental chip was actually at day forty-five. That first day where I felt normal would be where I would begin the next phase of recovery and the continued march to cure. The time where I mentally stepped onward to the six-month mark.

This period is still a dangerous time as was the last phase right after the five-day acute withdrawal ended. For now, the cravings are there and frequent but not constant like up to that thirty to sixty-day mark. If the recovering addict thinks he still needs to stay away from people, then he does. For myself, I did go out a few times when alcohol was present. It still wasn't easy to see the beer glasses frothing on the tables and bar counters. On my sixth month, while hiking the John Muir Trail, I was at a resupply campground one night. A group of hikers I was hanging around were standing at the campfire, drinking beer. I had a giant craving that lasted for hours. Probably because I was carb depleted, due to the hiking, and my brain remembered the easy source of replenishment in the form of the liquid wheat. But every time you have a craving like this, you remember the pact you made—and remember it is non-negotiable. Then recall the first five days of sobriety in the acute withdrawal phase. Do you seriously want to chance having to go through that hell again?

Once you decide you're in phase three, whether it is thirty, forty-five or sixty days, you hone in on the holistic program. Start cutting the sugar to very minimal levels. Now, I'm not saying you can't have a dessert, even every day. But I would make that indulgence once a day at most, a habit I still follow well over ten years out. Because like everyone else, I like ice cream and other sweets. And if you did use cigarettes, like most of us who dropped the barley did, then now is the time to quit them. I gradually cut down to three a day, and then in one shot dropped them. There were times later on, I picked the habit back up for a few weeks. These were usually stressful times, which enhance the old cravings for alcohol to surface. I don't recommend using cigarettes for stress. I did and I shouldn't have. I'm a one hundred percent nonsmoker today.

The diet should now be enforced with vegetables and fruits as well as comprised with good protein and grain carbs. Even non-alcoholics feel terrible if they eat fast food all of the time. The clean diet and lots of water are the weapons to fight the long protracted withdrawal. Anything that makes the body feel good throws a right cross against all that is trying to make the recovering addict feel bad.

Exercise should now be introduced and built to five days a week. If you had time to drink every night, you now have time to exercise. And you add the meditative program as well. I recommend things like Tai Chi, Qigong, Zen meditation and yoga. Or a combination with mix and match of the above. You exercise, come home and then do twenty minutes of the meditative stuff. New Age music around the house also calms the mind. Herbal teas aren't a bad idea either. A comprised holistic program is in the appendix. Another book I have written, for anyone, whether alcoholic or non-alcoholic, goes into much greater detail how to reconstruct your existence. It is titled, *Reinvention of Self: How to Change Your Life and Being Forever*. It is an excellent guide for an alcoholic to use as he is re-creating his life on all fronts.

Weekends will remain to be a challenge as there is that open time when you aren't at work. During the third phase, I remained to find the more intense cravings took place on the weekends. This makes sense as I had neurological memories of drinking to the greatest excess on the weekends. Outdoor activities can fill this downtime. Hike in the warm months or ski in the cold ones. If you aren't an outdoor person, then take up a hobby. Become an artist. Learn the guitar. Or teach yourself to become a day trader. Something that can fill the hours when you aren't at work.

And no matter what—keep reminding yourself that the contract you made to never touch alcohol again is non-negotiable. You never let the debate even enter your mind. You don't feel a craving and then battle whether you should drink or not. You feel the craving and understand that you will feel it, and it will pass. After about five hundred, it will be easy to disregard them. The ability to ignore cravings only grows with time.

CHAPTER 6

WALKING ON NEW TERRAIN

I had descended the Whitney Portal Trail, coming from the highest point in the Continental United States on the day of my six-month mark of sobriety. The peace that settled was tremendous. When I began the acute stage, I couldn't fathom even a few weeks without alcohol. It was incomprehensible that I was never going to open a beer can again, never taste that bittersweet wheat. Never get numb. Now, I could not only envision that lifestyle but accepted it as a new, ordinary habit of my existence. I could now see sobriety as a lifelong custom. Where I would go to every get-together and drink a Coke. Or tea. I would never plant that twenty spot on the wooden counter in front of a barkeep again. Or milk a case at home.

After crossing the six-month mark, what I experienced was very much like a newborn being thrust into a world with which he is unfamiliar. Even the sages at AA regard the one hundred and eighty-day mark as a huge checkpoint. This milestone is where they say you have a good chance to remain sober. Then they decrease that probability by sending the former addict down a mentally and physically poor lifestyle. They flush his system with cigarettes, sugar, caffeine and constant negativity. Oh, and in case you haven't heard—relapse is part of recovery.

By now, the former addict isn't entirely cured but should be well into the process of turning his life into one of good health as described in the previous chapter. He needs to continue the program, all soreness and fatigue dissolved months ago, now replaced with the gym or runner's high of movement induced opiates versus the ones which were once dropped by the barley. The diet is repairing the damage done to the kidneys and liver. I only periodically felt tiny pins that were intermittent now in these organs. The meditative program should be in force. You might have a whole collection of New Age ambiance music by now that you play while sipping that chamomile tea at night. Six months—everything is swell at this point, right?

Not yet. Things are much better for sure. But the recovering addict can't claim cure just yet. He has a year to a year and a half until the protracted alcohol withdrawal syndrome has passed. Many in AA will state that the second year is pretty much like the first year. Of course, if you want to extend that syndrome, their unhealthy advice will undoubtedly take you there.

I have known others who chucked AA and went their own way. Some had the protracted alcohol withdrawal syndrome for only a year. Mine lasted the entire two. But I also had thirteen years of hardcore drinking and about a decade of moderate levels with intermittent binge drinking before that. And a severe childhood that rose to the surface during the recovery. I can promise you that the best chance you have for reducing the length of the protracted withdrawal syndrome is to live by the healthy points I addressed in the last chapter.

The "protracted alcohol syndrome" means that the brain and neurochemistry have not rewired themselves to operate normally without alcohol. Cravings will still exist and are many times very intense. And there remains the emotional roller coaster. But it is more like the children's ride at the park as the rises and drops are not nearly as severe now.

The twenty-four-month mark, where the protracted withdrawal ends, is still filled with the turbulence that hits with varying frequency as you cross the skies into the horizon of cure. Sometimes the bumps are mild, and sometimes they lift you out of your seat. Periods of dark depression will continue to descend—and pass. Periods of anger will surface—even blind rage. More than anything, there is an intense feeling of disconnect and phobia to people that all recovering addicts experience. Everyone else had been living in the normal world all these years around me. My world had been chemically altered. All social interactions, even with close friends, were under the effect, all conversations a mild haze.

Prior to quitting alcohol, there wouldn't have been a single time in well over a decade with my peers, outside of work, that wasn't influenced as the liquid grain absorbed into the tissues of thought. I reflected about that factor a great deal, years later. There were friends that I lost after I crossed the cure of the two-year mark. It wasn't because all of them were addicts. It was because I found nothing in common with them anymore. I realized a few were pretty toxic and had been the entire time I knew them. I just never realized it as when I visited them, I was always at least half-drunk.

An addicted individual had entered the inferno six months ago. And now a stranger walked the long miles toward the gate of cure. He saw brief glimpses of the sun-filled meadow as the dark forest began to thin.

And sometimes an angry bear will grab and shake you as you make your way out of the woodline. Panic attacks were frequent in the protracted withdrawal stage. The former addict will experience a great deal of these episodes in the next year and a half. The attacks will be less in frequency years later, but they will still come. I would say at present, well over a decade sober, I probably have one every two to three weeks. They usually only last a day now at most. My holistic program beats them down and holds the attacks at bay. It is one of those things that the former hardcore addict is just going to have to live with for the rest of his life as a side scar from the prior longstanding addiction.

A panic attack is nothing but a sudden deluge of intensified anxiety that falls upon a person, temporarily suffocating him. It can be as severe as even inducing shortness of breath at the peak of the event. The attack will generally begin as a mild sense of discomfort or nervousness that builds into full-scale terror, a few hours later, and then gradually subsides. The episode usually starts as the sun falls and by mid-evening has reached a climax that will recede by late morning after a night of fitful tossing and turning. The dark walls have a sense of closing in on the person during an attack. He may think about death and its non-negotiable terms as he lies in isolation with rapid breaths. The "night terror" is nothing more than a panic attack in the darkness.

Panic attacks will happen a lot in the first twenty-four months of sobriety. And they will periodically occur afterward as well. The key is to ride through them as you did the intense cravings at the beginning of the recovery. They will subside. Engaging in whatever meditative exercise suits you will help greatly. It won't end a panic attack but will reduce its symptoms and intensity. The herbal teas will aid as well, such as kava and St. John's Wort. And understanding it is the brain activity having a bit of a conniption fit, that's all. A great calming technique is simply knowing the internal chaos will go away soon.

Specific triggers will set off a panic attack, especially up to the two-year mark. The recovering addict needs to understand these triggers so he can keep the incidents down to a minimum. I was a contract physical therapist, which meant I changed job locations every three to six months. Also, I would disappear into the wilderness for four to six months on expeditions, such as the Pacific Crest Trail. After my first attempt on the PCT, which I failed due to a severe quad sprain and forecasted long recovery, I took a contract in Cut Bank, Montana. I arrived on a Friday afternoon in late September. On Sunday, around 2:00 p.m., a severe attack came upon me.

Within an hour, the mild claustrophobic unease had evolved to an almost mental breakdown. I paced the room as time passed, trying to read and watch DVDs. That night was significant as it was the worst episode I had encountered since the initial withdrawal, twenty months earlier. It was the sudden transition from the wilderness of the trail to society, even on the outskirts of a small town in Montana, that largely induced it. It hit its peak around 9 p.m. I wanted to jump in my car and drive away as fast as I could. North to Canada or southwest back to California. I had no destination, just a dreaded wanting to immediately vacate the house they had set up for me. I only slept a few hours before the first day of work. It finally let me go on Monday evening.

The place I had set to contract for eight weeks was not a good karmic clinic either. You could cut the tension in the air with a small scalpel. Another episode commenced the following Sunday. The effects were not as intense this round, but they still held until the next day.

These types of attacks are not only typical but can be regularly expected in the first two years. As I said, I once had an AA participant tell me that the second year of recovery was pretty much like the first one. I would agree with that assessment to a point. The addict is completely disoriented in his new world. But I don't think the twelve steps will reorient him to it any faster. Because if you're ten years sober and still reliant on AA meetings most nights, you haven't reoriented to the world—you're hiding from it.

Understanding the nature of the panic attack is another reason I reject the AA system of continuous recovery. I believe the AA program keeps the former addict in this constant state of anxiety. At close to the one year mark, I mentioned I attended two AA meetings in two days. I had brought a friend who was in serious trouble with alcohol. She wasn't convinced she was an addict. I wanted her to hear the stories so she would realize she was. And like I said, I told her never to return as the program was destructive. While at the meeting, they went through their usual telling of "their story," which was the same tale—they drank too much chronically and did stupid things while intoxicated. In one meeting you could listen to twenty different versions of the same yarn.

An individual sitting next to me was flapping away about his recent social gathering—a party he went to the previous weekend. He was two years sober, mind you. Parties involve alcohol, and he was a "recovering alcoholic." But in his mind, there was no cure for AA is adamant that no one can be cured. He saw this party as a threat. He relayed to the group that the day of the event, in the morning, the first thing he did was chant the *Serenity Prayer*. Then he called his sponsor. Then he went to an AA meeting to mentally prepare himself for the gathering. Then he went to the party for a few hours. He came home and went to another AA meeting to mentally come down from the event. Then he called his sponsor again. He then reviewed the twelve steps and *Serenity Prayer* again and then went to bed, thanking the Almighty he had been able to stay sober that night.

Good God, *really*? Does this sound like a normal interacting individual? He was two years from his last drop and viewed a simple get-together as if he crossed the winter Sierras on two broken skis. I had been sober for almost one year and had gone to a social event the week before as well. I just drank a Sprite and didn't worry about anything. And, yes, watching people drink cocktails incited a few cravings. They came and went, and it was no big deal. It was no big deal because I didn't make it a big deal. It had been a year. I had had a lot of cravings by then. I went home, had a chicken sandwich and went to bed. I didn't have a conniption fit the entire day about the matter. And yet, AA is telling the guy this is how he should regard all get-togethers. Because he is always an addict and who knows if he will be sober tomorrow? Two years out and he has to have an array of phone calls and meetings to socialize with friends for one night.

Does this appear like a mentally sound way to live? To exist with constant panic about everyday life? I guarantee he has far more anxiety in his sober life than I do today. He has programmed himself that he will never be cured, always a short hop back to the bottle. And, of course, what really helps his cause is always knowing in the back of his mind that relapse may be part of recovery. Outstanding.

I, however, learned to keep the anxiety attacks to a minimum. Keeping a daily routine helps. Staying away from nicotine will also aid your mental health. As I stated, in the first few stages, people will use cigarettes to get through the initial intense cravings. But later, the cigarettes need to be eliminated. The healthy routine of diet and non-intoxicants will keep the anxiety to a minimum. And the fourth phase at six months out is where you cement the holistically healthy lifestyle. Healthy living keeps panic attacks at infrequent episodes. And also—don't mentally turn a social outing into a big deal when it isn't.

I told myself I would never touch alcohol again the night I gave it up. And that was the only mantra I repeated to myself throughout the acute phase, the thirty-day phase, to the six-month mark and the long protracted withdrawal to two years. And I state it today whenever I get a small craving, which by now it usually is when it happens—short in duration and small in intensity.

There was no question whether I would drink beer at a party when I was a year sober. I wouldn't. I drank that Sprite, had occasional cravings watching others drink, and the cravings passed. I wasn't hysterical because I didn't make myself hysterical, unlike the hysterics at AA. And that's what they sound like most of the time—cult-membered hysterics.

I was well into the fourth phase of recovery at the second and last meeting of AA I ever attended. The circle of storytelling came to me. I announced my name and declared that I used to be an alcoholic. Remember, in a previous chapter, when I told you the AA members become enraged when you reject their failed methods? They were here as well. The room grew quiet. *Doesn't he know the protocol*, they wondered? *No one used to be an addict. We are all still addicts. Didn't he just hear yesterday the guy next to him talk about the party?*

Yes, AA, I heard it loud and clear. And I found his story about the party ridiculous. Then I announced it was my second meeting, and I was almost a year sober. There was dead silence in the room. I knew what they were thinking. *But how? He hasn't done the steps. He never got a sponsor. He doesn't have his six-month chip in his pocket. How can he still be sober without our protocols?*

Because I determined in my mind, I would be, AA. And this time there weren't any condemnations like in the AA chat room, months before. Sure, they were mad—anyone could tell that, including my friend I brought with me. But they didn't know what to say. A half an hour earlier, a twenty-five-year sober man, looking very tense, still going to AA every night, stated this was the only way. And yet here I was, sitting relaxed in front of them—one who defied their protocols and had accomplished what most of them didn't while using their twelve steps. They couldn't very well say my plan wasn't working. And I apparently was calmer than the guy next to me the other night with double the time sober. We left shortly afterward. And all of these years later, I still haven't returned. And I'm still sober. I'm cured now—long ago. I still go to parties. And I still drink Sprite. And it still isn't a big deal. Most times nowadays I don't even get cravings at social gatherings at all. I'm sober today because of the recovery program I built and secured in the second and third phases on the road to cure.

I beat the anxiety, or should I say kept it to a minimum during the long, fourth phase, by keeping to a routine. The exercise program was, again, a key component and still is today. If it were a gym day, I would go even if in the middle of a panic attack. I knew cardio exercise certainly wouldn't make the symptoms worse. The opiates dropped from the vigorous movement would only decrease them. More than once, I only experienced mild symptoms while they lasted by countering with exercise and an influx of Tai Chi afterward while drinking herbal teas. Yoga would be added a few years later.

The routine of exercise, meditative work and herbals also worked on the blackout depressions that hit when the anxiety took a union break. Depression will continue to be very common during the protracted alcohol withdrawal syndrome, even though you are reconstructing your psyche. The opiates still aren't normally coming from the brain yet. Sometimes depression was active when I was in the middle of my bag work for Thai boxing or lifting weights. There were times when it even lasted for weeks, usually in the winter. But it would recede eventually. I rode the tide out like I rode everything else.

Different areas of the country can affect mood as well. This point is a topic that the recovering addict should take good note of, not only in the first two years of sobriety, but for life. Of course, not everyone has the luxury of choice to live in the sunny and warm Azores, but be advised of what they call Seasonal Affective Disorder from lack of sunlight. This deficiency can screw up the psyche of non-recovering personnel not to mention those strolling their way out of the inferno of addiction. In Alaska, there were only a few hours of daylight in the winter. Non-alcoholics would suffer from Vitamin D deficiency and become sullen. The former addict, especially one in the first two years of sobriety, is at high risk for severe mood fluctuations from the lack of D in Seasonal Affective Disorder. I decided not to live in Alaska permanently for this very reason.

There seems to be a cumulative build-up for depression year after year in Alaska for a lot of people, addicts or not. I contract there at times but not full time. I also contract in Maine and can immediately tell the difference in mood from Maine to Alaska. In Maine, the winter may sit ten degrees below freezing, but at least the sun is out. I remember one contract ended in Alaska, and then a new one began in Bangor. I transitioned right in the middle of winter, but the difference was immense the second I landed in the new state. So if one is in this protracted withdrawal phase and thinking about moving up north, I would wait, if you could, until at least two years of sobriety have passed.

There may be a career change involved, but if a person can manage to have control where he lives, it can make things a great deal easier. It's been a long time since I was in the protracted withdrawal phase and I was past the two-year mark when I ventured to the rainy and dismal winters to contract in the southeast islands of Alaska. And today, I alternate between there and the northwest as well as Maine. I stayed clear of Alaska until well past that two-year mark for precisely that reason. I still have to ride out depressive symptoms when I am that far north in the winter. I maintain normality most of the time by taking Vitamin D supplements and keeping the routine of going to the gym and engaging in Tai Chi, yoga and meditation. And I keep that clean diet in force. The same habits I constructed in the prior phases of recovery.

But no matter what physical and mental routine you keep, staying active will get a former addict through the protracted two-year withdrawal much better than the guy who was heartily involved in the mantras and steps of AA. That person will continue to be a mental wreck. And when one remains a mental wreck, the chances of failing sobriety are only increased.

I would also recommend during that first two years to not engage in any major life alterations. This includes any major moves or career changes. Deciding on a whim to leave your wife of twenty years to reunite with your high school sweetheart isn't a prudent thought at this time. Your mind is going to have many periods in those first two years when it isn't crystal clear due to the neuro reprogramming.

But if you can keep consistent in the above routines of holistic health and try not to dive off the deep end in any area of your life, the two-year mark of calm will arrive. And you will have achieved the cure from your addiction.

The symptoms of these panic attacks and depression will come and go with moderate frequency from six months to two years sober. You have to accept that and ride it out when it happens. And every time you do, new strength is forged. The worst panic attack I had was the one described in Cut Bank, Montana. I survived it without going back to the bottle. I've never had one that intense since that time. So I can survive the rest that will emerge here and there in the future. A large wave comes at the surfer, and what does he do? He lays on his board, turns forty-five degrees and lolls over it as it passes. And then the sea is level once again. He doesn't fear the next wave in the distance because he has done it over and over.

Previously, I stated that today I might have a panic attack every two to three weeks. Okay, that sounds awful at first glance, but let's look at that time frame more closely. The longest they ever last is usually twenty-four hours, hitting a peak at four hours in and then very slowly subsiding into the next day. Many times, they don't last even that long now. With exercise and meditation, I can push them back to minimal intensities, more often than not, as time goes on in sobriety.

But let's say every two weeks I had one that did last twenty-four hours and would have this frequency for the rest of my life. That would be one day in fourteen. That equates to seven percent of my life. Ninety-three percent of the time, I'm fine. I would also say I have moderate to high depression twenty percent of the time now. This means eighty percent of the time I don't have depression. I'm a physical therapist by trade. In my twenty years of experience, I can promise you that my anxiety-ridden patients, as well as my depressive patients, do not have even half of those percentiles for feeling good. Because some doctor gave them medications that don't cure instead of prescribing my holistic program that does. Eighty percent normal is awesome for a prior childhood trauma victim and former alcoholic. I'm probably doing better than a lot of non-trauma and non-former addict adults. Name me someone who doesn't have some depression at periodic times in his life, and I'll show you someone who should invest in the lottery.

Why was I doing so much better than the panic-ridden guy who relayed his party adventure to everyone? Attitude toward symptoms answers why. Attitudes that I secured in the second and third phase and cemented as part of my life. AA had convinced him to embrace suffering as a normal part of life for someone who was always an addict. They had instilled a chronic fear of symptoms where the only safe house was in their rooms under their strict guidance. What did this guy's sponsor need to tell him in the multiple times he called throughout the day? Review the twelve steps? Chant the *Serenity Prayer* together? He can do all of that, but it still comes down to one straightforward item that determines whether he will remain in an addictive free life or not. That factor is willpower. The choice to not touch alcohol again. Meetings, mantras, sponsors and steps won't keep him from putting a bottle to his lips if he has chosen to do so. And if he has truly chosen not to then the rest is insignificant. Cravings and anxiety? Nothing but passing feelings that subside unless you turn them into something greater than they are. My attitude was that when I finally passed the end mark of protracted withdrawal, I was cured. My new status would be one who recovered and was *cured*. His was that of an addict—forever. Compare the two outlooks and tell me which serves the person better?

Could I be an addict again? Sure, if I *choose* to drink, I would become an addict again. I *chose* not to drink again. I said relapse wasn't a part of recovery. Relapse is relapse. I would finish the protracted withdrawal stage as I finished the acute stage, post-acute stage and the six month mark. Then I would go on with my life.

A great many will fall off the wagon in the first two years, even if they make the first six months; the point where AA and others state you have a *good* chance to remain sober. I would rather have a *great* chance of staying sober. And this chance of cure is the development of a resolute mindset. *That you are not and will never again be an addict.* Willpower. The fortitude of spirit. The understanding that the bad times will ebb and flow in the first two years and you will drift with these currents—and never touch alcohol, no matter what. No matter if you lose your job, are being sued or lose a close family member. In the first six months, the intense on and off cravings are the greatest danger. After six months, it is the old neuroplasticity that induces the cravings again at times. They will come more for the former addict because of the bumps of life that everyone experiences. And every time you get through one unscathed, then you are only stronger for the next one down the road. It is also pertinent not to build up events in your mind, which may trigger cravings such as that AA member's party, which caused him so much undue stress. These events come and go, as well. They aren't a threat because of a mindset that is comprised of non-negotiable resolution.

Mindset. The human will is an incredible force. Once you plant it in your mind that you will never drink again—and believe it, you are on your way to freedom, regardless of those bumps in the road that you periodically drive over. And the first twenty-four months, you are still in protracted withdrawal. Maybe you don't go out much during that time. I rarely did. If you do go to a party and the cravings arise and seem to be out of ordinary control, you can always leave the gathering. For down the road, it will not be as bad as time continues to pass. Was the guy sitting next to me in that meeting going to go through his AA ritual in another two years every time he went out where there was alcohol? Or how about in six years? Twenty? If he has to engage in this nonsense, then he isn't free at all.

From month six to twenty-four, depression will be part of your life. And it will pass. You will have long periods of agitation. It will pass. Anger and restlessness will be common. They will pass. Periodic panic attacks will be a part of your life. They will pass as well. But there will also be large blocks of time when the person feels decent. Normal. When he will be just glad that he no longer wakes up sick every morning now. The fourth phase isn't nearly as bad as the first two or three phases. There is a lot to embrace, those many blocks of time that you are feeling good. And you will make yourself feel good in greater frequency by exercising, healthy diet, elimination of toxins and the spiritual recovery that I have set on you to embark. Or you can feel jittery on nicotine and caffeine, rehashing your past, locked away in the rooms.

As I was nearing the twenty-four-month mark, I couldn't even imagine any longer waking up to an ill, self-induced hangover. My nights were now routine with exercise. Any other time was filled writing my novels. I no longer thought of going to a liquor store. My diet was solid. Periods of peacefulness were becoming the norm. Any thoughts of alcohol were much milder as was periodic wanting for it. Time had negated the force of the cravings.

On January 22nd, 2011, I was in Helena, Montana, a little over a year away from my second attempt on the Pacific Crest Trail. I still rarely went out. Even when going to restaurants, I ordered the food to go. I had an almost phobic dread of being around people. Most of the time, I was a recluse. But I had reached the twenty-four-month mark. Two years. When I officially announced to myself that I was cured of the addiction. The second and last AA meeting I had attended was eleven months into sobriety.

As years passed, every once in a while, I would talk to someone I ran into who was in AA. They had nothing to say now, only this stupefied look when I told them I had neither taken a drink nor attended their meetings since I began my path to what I stated was a complete recovery. What could they say? I wasn't drinking, and most of them in their program went back to the bottle eventually. When people asked me why I didn't drink, I casually told them the truth. I told them I used to be an alcoholic. Now I'm not. I was cured.

That's right, AA. I'm *not* an alcoholic anymore.

I am *cured.*

SYNOPSIS: FOURTH PHASE TO TWO YEARS

After six months have lapsed, the initial tidal wave of anxiety and cravings will have passed with it. This doesn't mean that the emotional roller coaster or the cravings end. Not by a long stretch. It means the amplitude has decreased. The brain and neurochemistry will need to rewire itself. And that time to do so will continue to result in bouts of anxiety, depression and cravings for alcohol.

The holistic program should continue—and it should continue for life as well. The recovering addict needs to ingrain exercise and clean diet into his daily life as habit by now. The spiritual or meditative program should be routine as well. The more one continues with the holistic program of recovery, the less the frequency of cravings occur. The program will also lessen the effects of depression, insomnia and anxiety as well. The AA sponsor I had met in those brief encounters in their rooms once told me that the second year is a lot like the first. This opinion was valid only to an extent with me. My graph chart would have shown a progressing and steady line of recovery that second year as well. My cravings decreased by the month as well as insomnia and depression during the second year.

The cravings should now be dealt with easily. You simply continue to ignore them. You have done this so many times by this point that it should be automatic. You maintain the original contract that you made with yourself on day one. You keep to the fact that you will never touch alcohol again. Under no situation or circumstances will you break your oath. And you keep following that pact.

If you are able, try to avoid major life changes in those first two years. Your brain has enough to deal with in the protracted alcohol withdrawal phase. Try to avoid living in seasonal affective prone areas of the world. If you must live there, then be sure to use Vitamin D to counter the effect and utilize the continued holistic program.

Recognize the panic attacks for what they are. Use the meditative program to counter them. If you feel one coming, that is an excellent time to go to that gym—or take a brisk walk for thirty minutes. The episodes can be minimized or even reversed at times. But realize they are transient as well. You ride them out just like you do the cravings.

You should be able to go to a party and just drink Sprite or juice. If the cravings are too much, you may have to leave early. You may have to self-isolate at times in the first two years. This need for reclusion won't last forever. Eventually, the habit of not drinking alcohol will become so ingrained that you really won't think about it, even when everyone else is indulging.

Twenty-four months is when the recovering addict should now state that he has recovered. He can proclaim that he is cured. The rest of his life is merely continuing the habit. And it should be a life of tranquility from that day forth. In the next chapter, I will describe the contrasts between my program to cure compared to AA's program of forever continued illness.

CHAPTER 7

WHY I AM RIGHT AND AA IS WRONG

At the two year mark, the recovering addict can release himself of the title. He can now proclaim himself to be cured. He is no longer an addict.

That bold statement is my opening bell to the AA mantra. Everything else in my philosophy, versus AA's, follows from where that fork in the road splits. AA takes the turn toward never ending recovery, never ending meetings and a prison where the addict may never hope to be free. If you mention the word *cure* in an AA meeting, the hydra-headed response fills the room with a chorus of condescending anger. The anger is a knee jerk reaction of the statement that you will not reside on their plantation.

Can someone who is sober become an addict again? Sure, if he breaks his contract of never touching alcohol again. Just like a former smoker can transform right back to a current smoker if he lights one up. But after two years, it remains a simple choice. The same as it was during those first two years. The neurochemistry is now balanced, and the cravings will mostly be very transient and infrequent from this point out. There is no reason the former addict has to be sick again. Because he never suffered from a disease. His illness was only from an addiction.

This chapter will clearly show, side by side, the differences I have been speaking of between the failed AA philosophy and mine, which proved great success. I have mentioned many of these items of contention throughout the book but really want to drive home which strategy resembles logic and which doesn't.

So the first point of contention I have with AA is the end goal. They don't have one. I do. I say loudly and clearly that one can cure himself. I'm living proof that one can fully recover and never use the twelve steps as a guideline to orchestrate the rest of his existence. And on top of that, I am living a much more mentally and physically healthy life than what I saw in their rooms the two times I strolled in.

Another item I take great offense at is the AA mantra that relapse is part of recovery. I made a contract never to drink again. I had tried multiple times to quit in the past. But only when I took my vow never to touch alcohol again, no matter what the circumstance was in my life, was I able to find my road to cure. The "relapse is part of recovery" nonsense actually grants the participants permission *not* to promise themselves to abstain from alcohol for life.

Now, as I mentioned earlier in this book, AA will argue that this isn't what they mean—what they mean is only the person has to hit rock bottom before he is ready for the transition to an alcohol-free life—if he accepts their program. But go to a meeting sometime to see what I'm talking about. They talk about relapse around their circle. People are in and out of AA as they relapse, get clean, relapse again or "screw up" as they put it and then work those steps which continue to have that failure rate. And again, no one should have to "hit rock bottom" first. Wouldn't it be great if someone caught the addict midway through the addiction and showed them why they were drinking? Helped them rectify that childhood and make the compact right there to start living healthy?

AA is telling them it is normal to fall backward and then begin their imbecilic steps over. Once an addict goes through the misery of acute withdrawal, he should never want to participate in that walk on the coals ever again. And my program states you never have to. AA's states you may drink again, and that is normal for recovery. My program states that I know, for a fact, I will not be an addict ever again. Their protocol states you only know about today. Tomorrow is a maybe. The mind tends to follow a resolute command. AA has not given one. One is not issued because they have stated clearly that recovery never ends. I say you develop the mindset that you do know you will be sober today, tomorrow and years from now.

This mindset of "the rooms" brings me to another contention. Do you think it is mentally healthy to keep calling yourself an addict for life? Is it positive to state you will always be sick? That you will always have a disease? There is a wonderful psychiatric term out there, AA. It is called self-esteem. AA not only doesn't build self-esteem but actually takes it away from the person. The indoctrination that they provide is that the addict will never be a normal person again. And that philosophy is rubbish. I don't tell people I'm an addict. I say I used to drink—a lot. I may reveal that I was once an alcoholic. And that I'm not anymore. My program offers a spiritual rebirth where one truly regains his soul. AA provides the master status of the forever addict. One who will never be whole.

Added to the lack of self-esteem in AA is the severe negativity with every meeting. I can genuinely say I have never seen a group of people so trapped in their past. If you go to a support group for people who have lost a loved one, it is a temporary phase. You talk about it, get it out of your system, listen to others who have gone through the same thing, and one day you stop coming to the group. Because you no longer need it. You recover from your grief. Why AA believes they should continue to tell their stories of their rotten former lives every meeting, month after month, year after year, is beyond me. How many times are you going to "tell your story?" Remember my "story" I mentioned earlier of falling on my face in Bavaria while walking home completely drunk? I don't think about that anymore since it was over a decade ago.

The participants in AA never move past their wrecked lives because they keep living in them. I saw a few people there, in the two meetings I went to, who had twenty years sober. And they stated they go to AA six days a week. Are you kidding me? Where they spend every night reliving their lives from two decades ago? No one is going to feel good about themselves reliving this nightmare every night. And this is supposed to remind the addict not to drink? If anything, it would drive me right back to the bar counter.

My program doesn't live in negativity. I thought about the "whys" and "how comes" in the wilderness that took me to the six-month mark. I started fixing the childhood problems and expunging the demons. I wasn't emotionally perfect after two years of sobriety. You only begin to recognize what was wrong in the first two years after you quit the alcohol. You are in the first steps on the road to fix those issues. But I had started the process, and every year that passed, I was stronger after the protracted withdrawal phase ended.

I focused on getting better in my recovery program, not reliving the past. I improved in my field of physical therapy. I got myself physically healthy again. Spiritually intact. I learned how to invest money in better ways. I learned how to be kind to people. Compassionate. And I'm fulfilling my dream as a writer. It didn't happen right at the two-year mark. But everything in my life improved every single year I was sober. I can't imagine I would have gotten where I have if I was still stuck in a church, surrounded by cigarette smoking tragedies who are still talking about their wrecked lives of the past. It's in the past, folks. Leave it there. My philosophy is very straightforward. *AA offers negativity, and I offer positivity.*

As well as the mentally negative environment, AA is not physically healthy. I used cigarettes, at the beginning of recovery, to deal with cravings and anxiety. And in a few rough patches of life, I have been known to burn a pack or two in years past. But I don't smoke today. I also don't spend my nights jacked up on caffeine and sugar. Sugar filled foods are in small doses for me, and caffeine is strictly regulated to a few cups a day. I know from long experience that a healthy and clean diet reduces cravings as well as decreases anxiety and depression. The AA intake at the meetings increases them. Feel free to read a medical journal about the effect of these toxins on the mental sphere if you don't believe me.

AA demands that you must start their twelve steps and continuously work these steps, many times regressing a few back and then continuing forward. At no time does the former addict declare that he has completed the steps and is ready to move on to normality. The steps are for life. I contend there is one step needed to recover—stop drinking and vow to yourself; *you will never start again.* My plan works for Born Again Christians as well as atheists. You take that one giant step. And the rest of my plan is recovery from it to the cure.

With these twelve steps, AA has you not relying on yourself but solely on God and admitting that you are powerless over alcohol. And demands you make accountability to another human being, which is a sponsor. My plan states the most significant person of accountability is yourself. My program declares you are not powerless at all over alcohol and you never were. You may be prone to addiction, but the simple fact is if you are drinking too much you damn well know you are. As I stated in the beginning of this book, I will not buy, even on sale, that one can drink three cases of beer a week or a pint of gin a day and not think there is a problem. People deny it because they don't want others to know they have an addiction due to fear of social stigma. But they know it—don't try to sell me the bridge over that river in Egypt that says they don't. The only person you have to make a contract with is yourself. As far as God—by all means, pray to Him, Her or It for strength. The rest is up to you, the recovering addict soon to be cured.

Finally, it is my contention that AA doesn't save your life—it steals it. After AA indoctrinates the newly sober into their program, the AA existence is the only life the recovering addict has. The meetings are for life. The person will never be able to go on vacation without knowing where "the rooms" are near the hotel. I'm not kidding here—many of these people stop by in meetings when they are out of town, always having the fear that they will fall back if they stray from the program too long. Ten years sober, and they are still afraid to step out and live life on their own. What sort of logic says you are ten years sober and still going to AA six nights a week? At that point you don't have an alcohol problem—you have developed an emotional addiction in your psyche.

The cult doesn't stop with just remaining a member of AA. The addict becomes a sponsor. He gets involved in committees. He goes to national conferences. He comprises his entire social world with nothing but negativity, which is constant, from other addicts. If there is a spouse, many times, the title will soon be an ex-spouse. Of course, many of them end up divorced. The poor spouse, who wasn't an addict, has nothing in common anymore with someone whose every facet of life is involved in AA. Then AA tells them that is just the collateral damage of maintaining sobriety. If one stays in that program then one will become a prisoner to it. I have known some who started AA, stayed sober, and after a year or two, finally left it. They maintained sobriety and felt like an elephant finally rolled off their backs. Simply put, by rejecting the AA life, they reclaimed theirs.

My program shows how to get through the first two years, reclaim your life, enhance your life and then continue the healthy lifestyle. You won't be a jittery, cigarette smoking, caffeine-induced, amped up "recovering addict" who never recovers while the tale of woe is repeated every night for the rest of your life. You won't lose your spouse due to AA shutting their door in your wife or husband's face. You'll gain health, strength and vigor of spiritual rebirth. AA will have you reliving the past forever. I say deal with it, and then leave it behind for good.

The method and anonymity of Bill Wilson and Dr. Bob Smith made sense in 1935. In their time when men were practically required to drink. As a matter of fact, if you didn't, there could have been brawl about the matter. I've mentioned the name "John Barleycorn" from Jack London's work on the subject where he wailed this was the hard truth back then. The world at that time considered men feminine if they didn't swig the rye and wash it down with the barley. During that period, I can very well see why men needed a place to run and hide every night. And that era wouldn't even acknowledge female alcoholism.

But times have long changed since then. Our society doesn't scrutinize men today about having a Coke without the whiskey. And it understands women can be alcoholics too. You don't have to hide in shame in the modern era. AA should have changed its protocols a long, long time ago, especially since they have such a colossal failure rate. Someone should have looked up those statistics of failure and possibly considered that the program doesn't work for most.

I've listened to the reasoning from the AA members why they have such dismal success rates. They state the people who fail weren't ready to be sober. The old relapse as part of recovery again. They state the addict wasn't working the steps. I say it doesn't matter what their reasons for failure are. No one is interested in *why* a business fails—only that it does. And I contend they should either modify their program or go out of business now. *AA, your program doesn't work for most—that's it, and that's all.* And AA is doing a majestic injustice to those who want to quit alcohol by telling them their program is the only way. My program worked. The Prentiss program in California has tremendously high *cure* rates as well. They also use the term *cure,* by the way. They have success, and AA has failure. It is that simple.

AA should modify itself into a temporary phase. The steps should be thrown out with *The Big Book.* They need to drop the nicotine, caffeine and constant reliving of their fall from grace. Over the first two years, there should be a weaning off AA for good. They should have a group for people recovering under six months and then at one year and then one for those who are about to go off AA in the near future. If they took the holistic approach, stopped destroying peoples' self-esteem and empowered the former addict, they would have tremendous success rates.

But they don't. They keep chanting the mantra—like a Moonie cult. They follow Einstein's old definition of insanity by repeating failed patterns of treatment.

Those are my contentions with the twelve steps, the rooms and *The Big Book* philosophy. I don't have to prove these critiques of AA. Their massive failure rates prove it for me.

CHAPTER 8

WHY YOU WERE REALLY AN ALCOHOLIC

There was one more landmark where the experts, both AA and non-AA, say that you will probably never go back to drinking. It is at five years. Now, people *do* fall off the wagon after five years because they chose to pick up the bottle again. But the vast majority who make it this far are usually fair to say will die sober. The contention I have is—do you want to *live* sober? Or do you want to be confined to the rooms the rest of your life? Because here is a trade secret—you don't need them anymore if you crossed five years, for sure.

I wouldn't say that the healing process of whatever caused you to drink in the past is complete in the first two years of sobriety. It may start there and be well underway, but the process will finish long down the road after the protracted withdrawal stage. And I have never met an alcoholic or former alcoholic who didn't have trauma, usually childhood oriented, in their past.

Ordinary people don't just start drinking and advance it to the heavy stages for absolutely no apparent reason. If that were true, then half of the college graduates would go on to become hardcore alcoholics. They don't. They may drink heavily for a few years, and then it tapers off back to the recreational as they outgrow the party life. The same concept occurs in the military for the vast majority of soldiers who enlist and stay just for one tour of a few years. They drink like mad Irishmen on an extended bender and straighten that bend once discharged into the real world. Wild drinking is normally an early twenties thing that is outgrown by the late twenties. So I contend that usually the alcoholic is numbing something from his past. And that past will rise to the surface once he quits.

During the first two years, I came to an understanding of why I had become an alcoholic. But I didn't delve deeply into the process of extinguishing the demons until well after the two-year mark. My trail was a little unique—I actually went on a trail for 2,007 miles, at the beginning of the second year in sobriety, to find the answers. As I said earlier, I was stopped due to an injury about five weeks from the finish line on the Canadian border at the end of the Pacific Crest Trail. This happened in 2010. In 2012, I started over in April from the Mexican border and this time completed it—end to end. It was on the second long walkabout of 2,660 miles where I began to find the inner peace and the answers on how to undo the damage that had occurred, especially between the ages of fourteen to sixteen. A memoir of the account can be found in my book, *The Shepherd and the Runningwolf.*

It was during the protracted withdrawal that I accepted I had no internal confidence, only a high level of physical prowess. It was during this time when I realized my so-called command demeanor was an illusion. In reality, I had nothing but defensive anger, built from childhood and had its sword raised to enemies who no longer existed.

A few years later, when I gave a myofascial release seminar for hiker injuries in Sitka, after completing the Pacific Crest Trail, I saw my own video of someone who *did* now have command demeanor. I was nearing the four-year mark of sobriety. It was evident that I had a very congenial confidence within me now. It wasn't a swagger from telling everyone that I was once on a long-range reconnaissance team in Military Intelligence. It wasn't bravado about my twenty-plus years in martial arts, the last sixteen in full contact Muay Thai. It was from knowing I was good at being a physical therapist and knowing I could captivate an audience with what I had become proficient at in this field thus far.

When I was younger, in my twenties and up to when I quit drinking, I wanted everyone to know I was a Thai boxer and had been on that military team. Like I was trying to give an advance warning to potential enemies. Somewhere after year two in sobriety and the completion of the PCT in 2012, I lost the need for all of that bravado, which should have died in younger man's shoes. I can't pinpoint the exact moment it occurred. I can only say I knew I had found real command demeanor while giving the seminar a month after the trail expedition ended, almost four years sober. And it has only grown stronger every year. It grows stronger while the anger lessens.

But that should be the mission after year two. The first two years, the former addict should only be trying to accomplish making it to the cure and physiologically healing himself with the holistic program I gave in previous chapters. As I stated, you can declare cure at year two. Then over the next few years, you fix what you found broken from your past. For me, after walking a total of almost five thousand miles on the two trips in the wilderness, I found the answer. For all those enemies who may have pushed me down this path. For the dysfunctional family I grew up in and the horrid grandmother I lived with. For the bullies in high school that kept me terrorized for almost three years. There was an answer to finally letting it go. I was a bodybuilder, a former fighter and a successful medical contractor. I even became a writer on the side. There was only one more thing I had to do to let those demons in my past die.

I had to forgive them.

It didn't happen overnight. But I realized something after year two. I was listening to a Tony Robbins video on YouTube. He said his abusive mother made him who he was today. Tony states that he fought his way out of a dysfunctional life as well. And he conquered the world. He reveals that he wouldn't have if he had lived an ordinary childhood with no troubles.

I now think I should find those once terrible boys from Saint Xavier High. I believe I should thank them. If I wasn't severely bullied, maybe I wouldn't have gone way overboard with Thai boxing or the military. But those endeavors made me strong enough to fight my way into physical therapy school and battle an entire healthcare system that is corrupt and unethical. Those skills I learned in youth weren't for who I thought I was supposed to be when I was twenty. I wasn't supposed to be some steely-eyed killer or C.I.A. gee-whiz guy. I was supposed to be a physical therapist. I didn't become a good therapist in spite of my past endeavors—I became one *because* of the training I had in those endeavors. My black past gave me the tools for a white future.

And this is what has to come to resolve now that you are cured. For whatever demons brought you to addiction. For once you can claim cure, after two years, a whole new person exists. You are now a sober person. You now have to resolve the past. You may need counseling. Or for myself, I just studied books on the subject of abused children.

It wasn't all completely fixed by year three or four, even after completing the

Pacific Crest Trail. At close to year five, I went to Thailand to train in my art in their country. For eight weeks I walked through hell at a Thai boxing camp at forty-five years old—the oldest there and by twenty years, standing next to most of the young fighters. When I completed the eight weeks, I had a tattoo placed on my left shoulder. The Hanuman. The Thai symbol worn by Muay Thai practitioners. The inked motif that represents the constant battle with the demon—the demons on the outside and the one in all of us. A few months after I returned, I ran a Thai boxing class in a local gym in Wyoming. The calm demeanor was even more present than when I gave the seminar in Sitka. It only grows every year now.

That was my way of solving the past. I also studied ways to reduce anger. I learned techniques to rewire the neuroplasticity in the brain to form paths of peace versus hostility. And I continued my exercise and holistic program. I still do yoga, Tai Chi and meditation when I come home from the gym. I practice kindness now as much as I can and am much slower to anger. The cured addict is a new person in the world. He has been reborn. So you teach yourself to grow up differently now in the next three years.

Now be forewarned. Cravings will still occur—sometimes out of nowhere. Millions of neurons make up the brain, these lines that remember the incidents that led to your former life of alcoholism. If there is a scenario that reminds one of the past life, it is assured that it will trigger the remnants of that former existence.

I remember when I was in Thailand. Almost at the five-year mark of sobriety. Even though my endurance had decreased, I was training in my old, long-time art with more speed and fluidity than ten years prior. I felt mentally and physically great. The diet was clean, the air was fresh, I was training relentlessly and the views on the island exuded nothing but peace. And I was nearing five years sober by now.

I had worked the corner for one of our fighters on the island of Koh Samui. After the fight, we went on the town. Suddenly, an unbelievable craving for a bottle of beer hit me. Of course, it did. When I was younger and engaging in school organized fights, drinking was rampant and chronic with me. And when I lived in Germany, out on the various towns clubbing, I drank like two running tiger sharks. The combination of club life on an island that was known for such and the fight scenario triggered the intense wanting for that sixteen-ounce bottle of beer. Or eight of them. I hadn't had a craving this amplified since around month two after the last drop.

So I went back to my trained mindset. I knew I wouldn't succumb because I had beaten the cravings so many times before. No matter what. It would be an uncomfortable night. And it would pass as would the wanting for that bottle. I walked with the young fighters, holding a cup of coffee instead of the beer. At the clubs, I held a bottle of water. I remember counting the hours until I would go to sleep that night. The craving stayed with me until I went to bed at 3 a.m. By morning, it had retreated. It happened one other time after another fight when I worked the corner a few weeks later on that same island. But my mindset was already resolved. I would indulge the discomfort but not the bottle—per my day one oath. I used the willpower to say no. That's all. Once you have it, you are unstoppable. AA says you have no control because you have a disease. Nonsense. I have complete control at all times. I refuse to drink from the bottle. Today, I wouldn't pick a bottle of beer up any more than I would swallow arsenic for fun.

But the roller coaster is mostly level now only with an occasional bump like the above example. There are still periodic depressions and anxiety. But much fewer occurrences in frequency. Once in a bluish moon, there will be a severe panic attack—usually if I change living scenarios. It lasts about a day or two. As I stated before, I also have milder panic attacks about every two or three weeks, usually on a Sunday, which lasts until around noon the next day. So most of the time I don't have them. If the worst I have in life is a few dozen of these a year, then I'm doing alright. And I have periodic depressive episodes at times. So what? Name someone in the world who doesn't have bouts of depression. A lot of this is a very normal thing called life. And most everyone else deals with it without alcohol too.

Judgment on past events becomes very clear after two years. The compensation strategies I had used, later in life, for a terrorized childhood became evident. I remembered my time in physical therapy school. I was an ill-tempered, bitter individual toward my classmates. Now granted, the medical field is construed of pretentious asses a majority of the time. But I would like to think that I wouldn't have been so angry about it if I had gone through PT school sober. They were kids, for Christ's sake, when I was almost thirty. Of course, they had no life experience. I reflect now that maybe I would have had more of a sense of humor about living in the ghetto for a bit. And I wouldn't have taken two years to get licensed after graduation—that's for sure. I saw now that staying in the Thai boxing school the majority of the nights instead of dropping out for a bit to get licensed was ridiculous. I should have immediately taken a course to pass the boards the first time and saved myself two years of misery on Michigan St. in Indianapolis. But my mind wasn't clear back then. I needed the status in 1999 as a fighter. The alcohol kept me thinking that way. Without it clouding my vision, I would have seen the light far before I did.

I saw many past relationships for what they were in my drinking days. And they were comprised of nothing but chaos. Alcoholics have trippy mannerisms from constantly being in a state of substance withdrawal. They have a nervy edginess throughout the day. It takes a few bottles of beer after work to return to mental equilibrium. That levelness lasts about an hour before the mind then becomes altered with intoxication. Ninety percent of the time the alcoholic's mind is altered from the withdrawal as the tide recedes, altered from the excessive alcohol itself or is unconscious. There is only the brief interlude of the first few drinks that makes the addict appear normal before the baton is passed and takes back off around the bend. And chaos attracts chaos in relationships.

I had a girlfriend once who drank a few glasses of wine every night. I began to wonder if she was a light alcoholic as it ran in her family. I would have never thought that while with her during my drinking days. Because she was a novice compared to me. I had dated other women where I thought it nothing that they put away four Seabreezes in two hours with only minimal mental effects. Because they had lots of practice. And if who I was dating didn't drink heavily, they had catastrophic lives. They say in the laws of physics, two negatives repel each other. That is true in physics. In people, they attract like polar magnets. Emotionally stable women do not seek out the jittery and constantly agitated men for future relationships.

So as far as the AA step for amends, that would come with clarity of past judgment issues. I didn't do any damage to anyone except myself. So I made amends for sure—with myself. And then I let it go. I acted many times like an ass while on alcohol. I did stupid things and had piss poor judgment. I'm not going to beat the hell out of myself for the rest of my life. I swept out the bones from my closet. My house is now clean. And I'm not the same person, so I'm not going to keep thinking about that other person who I finally buried with London's closest friend and mine, John Barleycorn. Only when you can gaze back with sober eyes, two years later, can you see how your nonsensical life appeared during the drinking days. Because what is normal for alcoholics isn't normal at all for everyone else. Non-alcoholics have a trait the alcoholic doesn't own.

Stability.

One would think that newfound stability in life is a good thing. But for someone who has never had it, he walks like the foreigner in an unfamiliar land. You can accomplish a great deal when you don't fill your nights sitting with Uncle Buddy. In 2005, I began the notion of becoming a writer and began my first novel. Four years later, I only had the first draft complete. Then I disowned my Dutch uncle. Two years after that, I not only had published my first novel but had written, edited and published a second short one. I had much more time to write now, even with my time taken in the gym.

I thought about my mindset in my drinking days versus the two-year mark of sobriety. And I contemplated a great deal about my entire past while walking the Pacific Crest Trail. In 2000, I had a six-round bout in Thai boxing with the senior student. A very dangerous opponent. I won that bout. You would think that person who fought with fierceness, strength and fortitude would have had total confidence in his daily life. But drive and physical skill aren't the same as mental assurance. I won that bout and continued dating terrible women. Because I didn't think I was good enough for better. I stayed as an assistant instructor at the Thai boxing school instead of quitting it which would give me time to get licensed as a physical therapist—the degree I just spent four years achieving. But I was afraid of losing the status as an instructor in a fight club. So the boards waited. None of these issues were clear until long after I put the bottle down for good.

The first two years of sobriety, I figured out what was wrong as a result of my past. The next three years, I spent solving those ills and finally built real confidence. The person I saw on the local Sitka television, which played the video of my seminar, had what I always sought in my youth—real command presence. These were the types of resolutions from my past I had to mend one by one once I claimed cure at two years.

I knew my physiology was growing more relaxed in the years after I considered myself cured of alcoholism. I could tell in my training on the island in Thailand. I no longer needed Ibuprofen to train as the body wasn't battling the chronic effect of alcoholism any longer. As I said, I amazingly daresay that I was actually faster and more fluid in technique at forty-five than thirty-five, when I threw in the towel of going pro. I don't fight anymore as I did in our unsanctioned, school-sponsored events in Indianapolis but usually teach a few nights a week wherever I am training today. My old coach used to say my largest problem in sparring and events was my inability to relax. I'm sure it was back then. Even while in training, I was drinking eight to ten beers a night after practice while living in the ghetto.

After the two year protracted withdrawal, with a mind that is now in equilibrium, you can begin to advance yourself. At your career, hobby, marriage, or whatever suits you. You no longer stay stagnant. For me, it was becoming the best physical therapist I could be and advancing my writing. The initial marketing campaign I started in sobriety paid off on my writing works as they sold steadily. I never thought I would sell my novels with any real consistency. When I started, I assumed they would fall into the great unread vault of vanity publishing and possibly could be read by an archeologist digging through the ruins of the Library of Congress a thousand years from now. But I was able to find the time to research and market while continuing to write. And this all does take a lot of time. But it's nothing compared to coming home every evening after work and sucking the suds down until midnight or later.

The transition from abnormal interaction with people to normal mingling is a difficult one in those initial post-alcoholic years. At two years sobriety, you look back and see that everyone you dated and socialized with was as chaotic as you were. Now you're not in bars with other alcoholics who reside on the same stool every single night. You go to social events and see people drink one or two cocktails as regular people do. I would watch them and realize how atypical I once was.

In short, you reintroduce yourself to the world by hanging around better people. You leave your fellow addicts behind forever. In AA, new addicts constantly surround you. And many come and go, remember, for AA says relapse is part of recovery. Many in AA date each other. Then one falls off the wagon and reaches out and grabs the other's arm as they plummet. It's perfectly fine to want to reach back and help someone once you are sober—long sober. But to be continuously bombarded with it on a nightly basis? It just isn't good for you, mentally or emotionally. They never leave the attitude that they are sick and an addict. And they wonder why so many fail. My advice is to stay away from that negativity.

At the two year mark, I quit buying books on alcoholic recovery. I had read seven at the end of the protracted withdrawal. All of them, except one, said I needed to be in the twelve-step program. The one that didn't claimed an eighty percent cure rate, long term, with their method. Again, that is the Prentiss clinic in Malibu. The others typically had former addicts' "stories" in print. The ones who made it through the protracted withdrawal using AA guidelines were still in emotional turmoil, years after their last drops. Of course, they were. Who are they hanging around? Recent addicts and veteran sages telling them they will never recover, they have a disease, and if they leave AA, they are doomed to failure.

Imagine trying to gain decent relationships with people while at the same time constantly fixating on the cult-like mentality of AA. They disassociate from the rest of the human race for "the rooms." The only walls that give them a sense of safety. Because they were programmed from day one that without these walls, they would be doomed. The *Serenity Prayer*? These people will never gain serenity or peace. They are running scared, terrified that this will be their last day sober if they stray away from the contained kennel to rejoin the running pack. Recovery has not happened for them on any level. The continual AA process of recovery traps them forever.

After two years, the protracted withdrawal is over. You have claimed cure at this point. You don't drink anymore for the years after. Years three through five are nothing more than simply following that contract you made the first day sober. The AA sponsor states it isn't that simple—that you need AA to learn how to live. As they all live confined in their self-constructed prisons. Well, my method is that simple. Any intense cravings one will have will be infrequent as in my case in Thailand.

The AA sponsor then cries about the possibility of returning to the bottle if you were to wander off at the two year mark. Of course, there is a possibility. There is the possibility I wake up one morning and think snorting cocaine is a grand idea as well. But I choose not to. Just as I choose not to drink ever again. It's that simple. Choice. Willpower. Mindset. After two years, the amount of willpower needed is minimal as the cravings are so infrequent. Life is much easier now through the next three years. And will remain so with the healthy diet, exercise and complete holistic transformation—spiritually, physically and emotionally. Or you can sit with self-proclaimed addicts in a highly negative environment for years on end. Good luck with that.

Depression and insomnia will still be periodic as well during the next three years. Sometimes these periods will last for weeks or months. These symptoms may continue at times in the life of the former heavy addict, even after five years sober. They will come and go. But I can tell you that with a regular exercise program and healthy diet, combined with meditative work and herbal teas, I feel fine about seventy to eighty percent of the time. I can live with seventy to eighty percent and ride out the aqua blues when they come. I know people on antidepressants who are only mentally sound twenty percent of the time—until the med wears off. I have yet to take an antidepressant pill.

I would say the worst time I had between years two and five in sobriety was when I moved to Laramie, Wyoming for six months. I landed there to market my recent writing works and suddenly fell into a catastrophic, lethargic depression. I took Vitamin D, thinking it was lack of sun from the winter as I arrived in December. I couldn't sleep at night and was constantly anxious. I kept my routine of going to the gym, herbal teas, meditation and Tai Chi. Finally, it just let go, almost overnight. I just assumed that maybe winters weren't going to be great for me in the northwest and that's the way it was. One day, I was investigating real estate in the area and noted the elevation of the town. It was over seven thousand feet above sea level. High altitude leads to insomnia and anxiety for a few months until the person becomes acclimated. It was an unexpected bad time and I simply rode it out.

Personal catastrophic events happen to everyone but will always continue to be a threat to the recovered addict. Even the longtime, grand twelve steppers in AA, when under duress, may fall off and plunge from the wagon face down in the dust. In turbulent times, one must remember the vow he took the very first day of sobriety. The promise that he will not touch the substance again for the rest of his life. But things of a traumatic nature may still occur, just like with everyone else. And it *may* be traumatic. The event could be a divorce, loss of a job or even the death of a spouse or child. The demon will stir in his grave and a faint whisper will rise through the long covered dirt that the alcohol will just be temporary to make it through the hardship. The exact same mental mechanism that led to the abuse in the beginning of the addiction. That is why it is incredibly important to keep the mindset of one who may be in recovery in the beginning but *will* recover in the end. Versus the programmed mantra that one is always recovering, going up and down the steps but never getting off the ladder. I mean, really, why not drink away turbulent times if you are in AA? After all, relapse is part of recovery. What are you if you aren't always in recovery—if you are an AA member? For if you are cured, then I suppose there is nothing left to do.

And that is the point. After the protracted withdrawal period of two years ends, there isn't anything left to do except one last item. And it does stay for life. You don't drink again, no matter what. You put in your mind that if you lose your job, your wife, your kids and your house, then you sit with a cup of coffee on a street corner—sober. You don't touch it even in the worst-case scenario.

With these hard events will arise the cravings. And the cravings will pass as the hard times do. The cravings are their own entity now. If you ignore them, they will retreat. If you start negotiating with them, then they will prepare the brain for the intoxicant and become stronger. This mental wavering is how people fall into addiction again. They start thinking *maybe I can drink just a little* instead of shutting it down with *I never will again*. The latter mindset will form neural pathways of resilience.

Here is another example of one of the strongest cravings I had after the two-year mark because of life events. I had returned from the completion of the Pacific Crest Trail. I had greatly contemplated, on the expedition, my very difficult childhood which overflowed into adulthood as well, coupled with alcoholism. A great deal of my past was resolved on the 2,660-mile trail as I portray in my book, *The Shepherd and the Runningwolf*, about the journey.

Literally hours after I completed the trail, I opened an email from my brother who had been trying to contact me for weeks. My mother had been diagnosed with stage four breast cancer. I found later that with treatment the prognosis was two years. A month after this news, I found, by a gut feeling and an internet search, that my very abusive grandmother I lived with, from sixteen to eighteen, had finally died. Between the two events, my childhood again rose to the surface. Even though I hadn't contacted my extended family for well over twenty years, it brought to ground level the realization that I had no family with whom I was close. And that the last remaining string was about to be cut by the knife of cancer with my mother.

I was house-sitting for a friend in Sitka, Alaska for a few days, right after the news of my mother's stage four cancer and grandmother's death. They had a few twelve-packs of beer in the cupboards. Suddenly, out of nowhere, the cravings hit as intensely as if I had just quit drinking a week ago. This episode happened even though I was nearing four years of sobriety. Nothing was working to reduce them—not my Tai Chi or other breathing exercises. But what was my vow, I thought? Yes, these were difficult things to deal with in my mind. Everyone has difficult things to deal with at times, every day all over the world. The cravings were there, but the option to drink in my mind never was. There was no option because I had made it non-negotiable long ago. I didn't believe relapse was part of recovering. I was recovered and cured. And I was going to stay that way. I left the house and went back to my apartment. And the craving passed. I knew it would pass because I had been there before.

When you don't give the craving an acknowledgment, it has no choice but to fade from whence it came. The next few years were emotionally difficult. So is a recently divorced woman's existence, who may now have to raise children alone. These difficulties are known as *life*. The seasonal darkness the following winter in Sitka didn't help my mood. Recurrent depressions were greater in frequency that year. The high altitude transition to Laramie, Wyoming brought mood changes as well the year after that. There was also euphoria—like when my first novel began selling steadily, and my blog began to gain a small audience. I rode through all of it, the highs and lows, without alcohol.

I kept my program of exercise, clean diet, meditation activities and Tai Chi as key components. There were bouts of depression even so. When you're not close to a parent, who is now dying, a combination of anger, guilt, resentment and relief of coming closure flows through your soul daily. A former addict is not unique with these travesties. You could walk down any block, anywhere in the world and find someone with the same story. The difference is they don't drink the pain away, like you used to. And now you don't either. You must resolve to keep it that way. You deal with it just like your neighbor down the street. He's not getting drunk every night, is he?

The soul will finally break free if you keep a healthy physical and mental regime. As I stated earlier, the high altitude, sudden isolation of sitting in an apartment to focus on writing and marketing my novels, while thinking the end was coming for my mother, threw me into a tailspin for about two months in the winter of 2013-14 in Laramie, Wyoming. I wanted to take up smoking again, as well.

But I didn't. I kept going to the gym and doing my meditative work. I followed a decent diet and used the herbal teas. And the black fog eventually vaporized. It was a bad two months. And I don't think I would have felt one bit better if I spent it night after night in an AA meeting with a circle of people telling me I was sick and would never be cured as I regurgitated the story of my prior life over and over. Was that routine supposed to make depression go away? Would it make me feel better? I contend once more that the negative environment of AA will only tempt the person to go back to the bottle and become an addict again.

This next thought will be the conservative side of me speaking now. You have problems. They are real problems, for certain. And everyone else has different versions of the same problems. What makes you special? You used to drink. Now you don't. Other than that, all of the amp'd up crisis scenarios that AA says you can't handle alone are no different than everyone else's who live on your block. Of course, you can manage them. You just handle them without drinking—as does everyone else. Bad times come and bad times go. AA is not going to make your bad times better. A part of your life will consist of having periodic cravings when these bad times come. Don't acknowledge them. No negotiation. You aren't an addict anymore. AA says you have no control over a disease. Sure, you do. You have all the control, and it isn't a disease. It *was* an addiction. Someone should have told you that day one into sobriety. If someone would say that, it's possible AA wouldn't have the miserable failure rate they do.

You have a choice. You choose not to pick up the bottle again. Ever. You don't need a big book of guidelines on how to live your own life. You finish this small book, and then go live it. Who told you your life belongs to a program that destines most for failure? Your life wasn't meant to be spent in the rooms every night. It was meant to be lived—by you.

When I had passed the four year mark, the days of hangovers and vertigo in the mornings were now distant memories. I couldn't imagine living that way again. All I had to do was think about the daily elevator ride in the hospitals I worked in, years prior, with the a.m. weaving in my head. That was enough to make me never want to pick up the bottle again. Of course, I wasn't going to live that way again. I wasn't reliving it every night, sitting in the AA circle either. Was it tough dealing with the recent news of my mother? Sure. Was I going to pass that time with morning vertigo and a knife in my side every day? No way.

I remembered what the long-time AA member said in one of only two meetings I ever attended: *This is the only way to stay sober. The twelve steps. You will go back to drinking if you don't follow them and come here. This is the only way.*

And I bet he is still there—trapped in a perpetual recovery that will never end. At the end of his life, he will be able to say he spent it in a smoky room, terrified he wouldn't be sober the next day. And here I was—four years sober and had not completed a single one of their steps. I started with a rejection of step one. A higher power existed—of that I was certain. But I wasn't helpless. And I'm pretty sure the higher power didn't want me to be either. We aren't helpless, and alcoholics aren't diseased. We have something known as human will.

The last line of defense from AA is: *but there are people we help. We have people that are still sober.* You have people who became sober while in your program, that's true, AA. How you've helped them is largely up for debate. AA states they teach people how to live. After about a year of sobriety, that was the mantra I heard when I would run into someone from the rooms. They would tell me it was great I made a year but still needed to start their twelve steps. That it was necessary to learn how to live. I couldn't live on my own without them.

AA doesn't teach you how to live. They teach you only how to exist; locked away in their meetings for the rest of your life. They offer an existence in perpetual fear of ever leaving the reservation for independence in the real world. In their world, you sit in the circle, telling your story forever. And the simple fact remains that no matter what their rationale is, most of them go back to drinking anyway. Of course, they slide off the wagon. Their wagon of recovery was missing a wheel before it ever started forward.

I'm not incredibly interested in AA's reasons why they have such dismal failure rates. *The person hasn't hit rock bottom yet. Relapse is part of recovery. He wasn't ready for the next step. He didn't keep in touch with his sponsor enough.* It doesn't matter why. AA fails most. And that's it, and that's all. So why do people keep going time and time again? Because we haven't evolved enough to realize the protocol is broken.

This was the same mentality when we used electroshock therapy for psychiatric conditions as standard practice. Remember electroshock therapy? It wasn't discarded that long ago by the psychiatric community. The high powered experts completely believed in it at the time, just a few decades past. And then one day someone realized the results weren't there. They finally acknowledged out loud the procedure wasn't curing people at all. So the protocol was abandoned. Now we dope everyone up on medications for depression and anxiety and all of the various ailments that are attributed mostly from this thing mentioned before called *life*. Decades from now, we will realize those tactics were failures as well.

My point? Just because Bill Wilson and Bob Smith started a program almost a hundred years ago, that no one altered in all of this time, doesn't mean it's effective or right. The Prentiss clinic in Malibu has disregarded the AA mantra. They claim to have an eighty percent cure rate. That's correct, AA—*cure rate*. The cult mantra shouted from the rooms doesn't change the very uncomfortable fact that they fail and Prentiss succeeds.

What can you tell me to defend yourself, AA? Can you make the periodic anxiety that comes and goes with former alcoholics disappear? No, you can't. Will going to your rooms cease the intermittent depression that rears its head at times? No, it doesn't. Can you keep me from ever having a panic attack if I walk your steps? You can't. Will cravings disappear forever if I put *The Big Book* on my shelf? No, periodic cravings will still come—probably for the rest of my life. The choice is to learn to live with the above or hide from the above—which will still find you whether you are in the rooms or not. I choose not to exist as a slave to AA. I choose to live on my own terms.

I looked at my clock on January 22nd, 2014, in my small apartment in Laramie, Wyoming. The town I chose to reside in while finishing my third book about spiritual recovery on the Pacific Crest Trail. The hand eventually moved to 11 p.m. Approximately the time I threw the last few beers into the trash in my former apartment in Turlock, California. Where twenty-four hours later, the hell of acute withdrawal would begin in force. I had made five years since that night. I had taken sobriety with me through California and Montana. On the trail from Mexico to Canada. Alaska. Thailand. And then, Wyoming.

According to all statistics, my chances of remaining alcohol-free were now very high. I didn't have any chips. I hadn't given any speeches to a circle or group. The day I completed five years, I had gone to the gym. I practiced my Tai Chi and engaged in my writing. It was just another typical day. Because my master status wasn't of an addict. I wasn't diseased. I wasn't sick. Alcoholism was part of my past. And the past is where I kept it. I had recovered years ago. I had beaten a vicious addiction. And I remained cured.

The only way I would be an addict again would be if I suddenly went out and picked up the bottle. And I wasn't going to do that ever again. Because after all the mantras and guidelines from AA are uttered, once one completes all of their sacred steps, it still comes down to one simple thing on whether someone will be an alcoholic or not.

Choice.

I looked out my window that night as the snow quietly fell. The universe silently acknowledged my five-year mark of sobriety.

My choice was final.

SYNOPSIS: AFTER THE CURE

Once you have completed the two-year cure mark, it will be time to resolve whatever caused you to drink at the beginning of your alcoholism. And I do not buy you just accidentally got addicted to the hops over time. How a person resolves their past depends on what happened in the past. For me, it was an acknowledgment that I had been living an illusion of feigned confidence when I had only physical confidence, backed by military exploits and martial arts. So I began to build confidence—real fortitude that only grows and exists still today. And to do that, I had to let go of my childhood—by forgiveness.

I'm not a fan of shrinks as shrinks prescribe meds. Possibly counseling could help some—I've known a few good therapists from working in the medical field. I'm a big fan of Tony Robbins' work. That man knows of what he speaks. For me, I read a lot of Robbins' and other books. I amended myself. I continued the reinvention of a brand new person after twenty-four months of recovery. Again, I refer to my other work on how to change your life in a step by step process on all planes of existence: *Reinvention of Self: How to Change Your Life and Being Forever.*

Being a brand new person means you build that person from the ground up. Everything that alcohol kept you from doing before, you now engage in today. If you want another career, make that happen. Or advance yourself in the stock market. Or become a Big Brother or Sister to the youth. Do you want to make amends to the world? Then do something to make it a better place. I have taken three troubled souls over the years into my world of Muay Thai. One was a recently divorced fellow who was at rock bottom when I met him. He learned strength not from me but the art. He is now an RN—and happily married to another RN. I also advanced my writing. I finished my fictional, dystopian book, *The Second Fall.* It sold an initial few hundred copies and got some great reviews. Only later did I realize my real calling in writing was self-help for others. What strange and wonderful roads life takes you down when you obtain the cure from alcohol addiction.

You resolve the past and advance the future in the years after you make the twenty-four-month mark. And you keep the holistic program, given in the previous chapters, for life. You follow the Boy Scout Code: staying *physically strong, mentally awake and morally straight.*

Cravings will happen but much more infrequently. If a strong one comes out of nowhere, then you have had enough practice ignoring them that it should just be another day at the office. Remember your vow—and the hell of acute withdrawal. You cannot try again with alcohol to drink like a normal person when you know you were already an addict once upon a time.

Depressions and panic attacks also happen, but they aren't as intense or frequent. Keep the holistic program—and a sense of humor.

At this point, there is nothing left to add. You keep engaging the program and stay cured.

CHAPTER 9

LEAVING YOUR PAST BEHIND FOREVER

I look back today at the reflection I see in the mirror. The normal color in my cheeks. The relaxed features and serene eyes. I cannot imagine that I used to drink twelve beers or more a night. The shakes and vertigo in the mornings. Who was that person? He is a stranger now. I cannot comprehend that I lived in his shoes for thirteen years. Knowing that if I had kept on, I would now be having medical issues due to alcohol abuse today. Or I would be dead.

AA was right. I do drink today. My drink of choice is three to four cups of herbal tea. This is my new addiction. I still put away three cups of coffee a day as well. I chuckle at this. I have been saying for five years now I would quit coffee completely. Maintaining minimal levels of caffeine in my system is my fixation today. I want to defeat the coffee bean. I used to drink over three cases of beer a week. Now I concern myself with a few cups of coffee.

I stared at the mirror once, close to the five-year mark, that winter in Laramie. Was it possible I looked younger than I did five years before? I certainly looked more alive. And the needles of pain in my side and back were years buried as well. Nothing hurt as I completed thirteen rounds on the heavy bag at the gym and lifted weights five days a week. The gym where I taught a few students boxing and Muay Thai.

Every once in a while, I put in the DVD of my seminar I gave in Sitka on myofascial release. I see the relaxed demeanor of one who has no stage fear as he addresses a library full of people from the community for an hour. A confident, medical professional and public speaker has replaced the former shaky addict. The person orating doesn't need a numbing agent anymore. He doesn't need the alcohol anymore. His high in life is the understanding that he is well versed in his chosen craft.

Is everything perfect today in my life? Of course not. Who has a perfect life? I had a bad winter in Laramie as I passed the five-year mark. That lasted a few months. And then the winter retreated for the brighter spring. And when the occasional craving raised its head, all I had to do was think about the acute withdrawal I had gone through. I remember what it was like curled in the corner of my apartment, shaking. And then I recollect the protracted withdrawal that followed. Did I want to go through that again? Never. I would never go through it again because I had decided never to touch the substance again. And I kept my regime. Exercise. Diet. Herbal teas. Meditation, Tai Chi and later yoga. The program I continue whether I'm feeling good or bad. I continued it in that emotionally negative time in Laramie—and eventually sleeping patterns returned to normal and the depression faded.

But there will be other times, even twenty years later, when things aren't swell, I'm sure. And I will continue the regime that led to my recovery. Because leaving alcoholism behind isn't about walking through life diseased. It is about strolling through wholly cured. It is also the pursuit to recreate the person, a spiritual revolution.

One day, I'm in Laramie, in a coffee house. I'm about to leave a small town once again for the road as a traveling physical therapist. Spring has returned as it is May now. I was a few months into my sixth year without a drop of alcohol. I sat next to a woman who acknowledged she was in AA. She had noticed the topic of a book I was reading for research of this work and came over to my corner. Her eyes grew excited, a fellow addict she found in the land of the sober. The sun warmed the room and shined on the table, where I compiled my notes.

"How long?" she asks.

"I passed five years in January."

"Which house do you go to?"

"None," I reply. "I don't do AA." Her eyes are confused. How can I be five years out and not be in AA, she wonders? Almost as if knee jerk reflex, the chant, long indoctrinated in her since the first week, begins in force.

"But you have to learn how to live. AA teaches you how to live with sobriety."

"So they say," I replied. I don't even bother to argue—the mantra is too instilled. I look at her sadly. She isn't a bad person. After all, she wants to remain sober too. But she was programmed in her initial weakened state of the protocol and is now too terrified to think otherwise. She is too frightened to believe that she can live without AA. She doesn't realize that she isn't living by aligning herself with the rooms. She is merely existing—in the past.

They celebrate their chips for their time in sobriety. I celebrated turning forty-five, a few months earlier, by training in a Thai boxing camp, three hours a day, for eight weeks. One day, I rode on the bare neck of an elephant through the lush jungle of Koh Phangan island. Before that, I completed the 2,660-mile Pacific Crest Trail from Mexico to Canada. Stood at the northern terminus in late September as the cold winds of fall began to blow after five and a half months on the trek. I traveled through the Yukon, stopping to see the bison lined up next to the roadway. I once reeled in a thirty-pound salmon off Baranof Island and the town of Sitka.

I need to learn how to live?

I think not. Her life will be meetings in AA. Cigarette after cigarette, telling her story. She may be a sponsor herself now, chanting the maniacal mantra to a newly sober person who will also learn no other path except the prison of the rooms. She won't go on a vacation unless a meeting house is near. Her entire existence will revolve around AA. Sponsors, meetings, committees, everything is AA now in her life. Her master status is *I'm an addict.* Compare that life to mine today. Which sounds better? And use common sense. Is what I'm stating logical or illogical? Does AA have success rates that are significant or not? They don't. And that's the end of the debate.

They fail most.

And since they fail most, I can make the following statement. I don't need a degree in substance abuse counseling. No degree will match my experience. And no degree will counter AA's dismal success rates. Whether they like it or not, my next words are founded in truth:

AA, your entire philosophy is ridiculous. You don't help people; you hurt them. Your good intentions lead to another roadway toward a different hell. You don't teach them how to live; you imprison them. You make them afraid to live. You destroy their self-esteem. You tell them their master status is forever that of an addict. That they will forever be sick. Diseased. You destroy their relationships. Their marriages. And even after all of your sacrificial lambs' ashes are left smoldering on Bill Wilson's alter, you still fail. Wilson and Smith's program fails you. You need to modify your protocols. Your mindset. Because the bottom line, the only fact that matters, is your program doesn't work. And I don't need to prove my point. Your own statistics prove it for me.

You may need a haven initially to begin recovery. But you don't need AA to live. The only thing you need is you. Your willpower. Your ability to choose not to drink. You need a healthy lifestyle and mindset. You can recover. You don't have to be an addict anymore. You can find the cure. You can be just like everyone else a few years later. You'll just be a person who doesn't drink now. You have the same problems everyone else has. And you need to deal with them like everyone else. But you never touch alcohol again.

You have to reclaim the warrior within you. That's the difference for someone who stays cured and someone who doesn't. AA doesn't keep you from falling off the wagon, as a matter of fact, the risk is greater of tumbling when you are a part of AA. Most in the rooms choose to pick up the bottle again. No one taught them how to be a warrior. No one showed them the steps to recreate themselves. AA told them they were sick. And always would be. Completing their twelve steps won't help. It won't help because no one told them the one simple step needed for a cure.

That it is your choice alone to quit.

My name is Charles Hurst. I used to be a chronic stage alcoholic. It was really awful in the final years. The last few years of my addiction, I existed in Hell. One day I decided to quit. And that was Hell too. But it is over now. I passed ten years of sobriety, and I am still sober to this day. I'm not an alcoholic anymore.

I'm cured.

My name is Charles Hurst. I used to be an alcoholic. Today, I'm not. I reclaimed my life.

I hope you do too.

AUTHOR'S NOTE

I began this work at the five year mark of sobriety. Five years since that initial night when I stated I threw the last remaining beers into the trash. I was in Laramie, Wyoming at the time and had just launched the platform for my two fictional novels, *The Second Fall* and *The Monterians*. I was also in the final editing process of my memoir of the arduous trek on the Pacific Crest Trail, *The Shepherd and the Runningwolf*. Where I finished one trail and began another—a path of forgiveness toward the long ago tormentors in my childhood.

I have had the luxury of being an independent contractor with no obligations except to myself and have been able, over the years, to exit from the work force for extended periods of time. My time in Laramie was one of those exoduses. I had long decided by then that the entire philosophy of Alcoholics Anonymous was bunk. I felt this driving urge to counter their failed philosophy. Hence, *The Small Book: How I Beat Alcoholism and Why Alcoholics Anonymous Doesn't Work*, was written. The first draft was completed in a matter of weeks.

Between 2014 and 2019, I went through several crises. I lost a friend, who was more like a brother, to cancer in 2017. I lost my dysfunctional mother to cancer as well a year and a half later. I had grown to despise my career, seeing many more patients in physical therapy than not, who were victims of nothing more than their own poor lifestyles, resulting in chronic pain that could not be resolved. I managed to pull through these periodic dark times without returning to the bottle. The thought of drinking again never even entered my mind. My other work, *Reinvention of Self: How to Change Your Life and Being Forever*, was a direct result from these turbulent times.

On January 22nd, 2019, I crossed the ten year mark of sobriety. It has only continued today. I haven't had a debate with an AA member since that coffee house in Laramie, which I described in my last chapter. What can they really say? I'm well into my second decade sober and my mental well-being only grows in fortitude with each passing year. I am now half retired and continue the adventure path, many times spending vast amounts of time in foreign lands. I'm certainly not spending my days locked away in the infamous "rooms" reliving my past every meeting.

Bill Wilson and Dr. Bob Smith didn't do the universe a wrong by creating AA. But they should have had the foresight to modify their strategy. In modern times, the leaders of the old foundation definitely should have realized the dismal results that come out of their smoky rooms.

Alternative methods to achieve sobriety are beginning to surface, however. Periodically in the bookstores and Amazon you will come across *Non Twelve Step* . . . titles. Unfortunately, the amplified screams from the traditional programs still reign the market. It is my hope that one day AA will realize its failure and adopt new methods to reach a growing population that is having issues with alcohol abuse in greater and greater numbers. For if "traditional twelve step" programs continue to be the mainstream, many addicts will remain imprisoned by their failed protocols.

C.H.
December, 2020

LIKE THE BOOK? HELP SELF PUBLISHED AUTHORS BY LEAVING A REVIEW ON AMAZON. THANKS AND SAFE TRAVELS TO YOU IN YOUR LIFE JOURNEY.

OTHER WORKS BY CHARLES HURST

THE SECOND FALL

THE MONTERIANS

*THE SHEPHERD AND THE RUNNINGWOLF: A PATH TO
FORGIVENESS ON THE PACIFIC CREST TRAIL*

*REINVENTION OF SELF: HOW TO CHANGE YOUR LIFE AND
BEING FOREVER*